Touching People's Lives

Leaders' Sorrow or Joy

Don:
Nice seeing you
again —
Mike Losey
June 17, 2017

MICHAEL R. LOSEY

Touching People's Lives

Leaders' Sorrow or Joy

Society for Human Resource Management
Alexandria, Virginia I www.shrm.org

Strategic Human Resource Management India
Mumbai, India I www.shrmindia.org

Society for Human Resource Management
Haidian District Beijing, China I www.shrm.org/cn

Society for Human Resource Management, Middle East and Africa Online
Dubai, UAE I www.shrm.org/pages/mena.aspx

SOCIETY FOR HUMAN
RESOURCE MANAGEMENT

Also by Michael Losey

Tomorrow's HR Management
With David Ulrich and Gerry Lake
John Wiley & Sons, 1997

The Future of Human Resource Management
With David Ulrich and Sue Meisinger
John Wiley & Sons, 2005

The Seed: What Shall I Grow Up to Be?
CreateSpace, an Amazon company, 2014

The Michael R. Losey Excellence in Human Resource Research Award

Sponsored by the SHRM Foundation, this award honors lifetime achievement in human resource research. It recognizes an individual for significant past and ongoing research contributions that impact the HR management field. A single award of $50,000 is presented annually to further the field of human resource management. Nominations are encouraged for scholars with a significant body of work in the field of HR.

For more information, visit **shrm.org/about-shrm/Pages/loseyaward.aspx.**

Dedications

This book is dedicated to all of those who have touched my life.

Annie, my ninth-grade sweetheart and late beloved wife of 49 years.

Michael, where it all began.

My parents and mother and father-in-law, the finest of examples.

My sister, who keeps me from having a big head.

George Odiorne, Ph.D., mentor.

"Sunny Old Bob" Ressler, who taught me the style and value of credibility.

Frank Powl, a true gentleman and early coach.

George Delp, a great motivator and principled leader.

"Roomo" and his lovely wife, Lamoyne, for their lifelong friendship.

All of my many friends, co-workers, students, and others who have encouraged me to put my stories, values, and interests into a book.

My three children and their families for their loyal support and understanding.

Don Quixote, who taught me how to fight windmills.

Kate Herbst, SPHR, my encourager.

Deanna Gelak, President, Working for the Future, and congressional expert.

Nephew Mark Liparoto, for great insight and editing.

And Margo, my new life partner, encourager, and editor, who helped me greatly.

This publication is designed to provide accurate and authoritative information regarding the subject matter covered. It is sold with the understanding that neither the publisher nor the author is engaged in rendering legal or other professional service. If legal advice or other expert assistance is required, the services of a competent, licensed professional should be sought. The federal and state laws discussed in this book are subject to frequent revision and interpretation by amendments or judicial revisions that may significantly affect employer or employee rights and obligations. Readers are encouraged to seek legal counsel regarding specific policies and practices in their organizations.

This book is published by the Society for Human Resource Management (SHRM). The interpretations, conclusions, and recommendations in this book are those of the author and do not necessarily represent those of the publisher.

This publication may not be reproduced, stored in a retrieval system, or transmitted in whole or in part, in any form or by any means, electronic, mechanical, photocopying, recording, or otherwise, without the prior written permission of the publisher, or authorization through payment of the appropriate per-copy fee to the Copyright Clearance Center, Inc., 222 Rosewood Drive, Danvers, MA 01923, 978-750-8600, fax 978-646-8600, or on the Web at www.copyright.com. Requests to the publisher for permission should be addressed to SHRM Book Permissions, 1800 Duke Street, Alexandria, VA 22314, or online at http://www.shrm.org/about-shrm/pages/copyright--permissions.aspx.

SHRM books and products are available on most online bookstores and through the SHRMStore at www.shrmstore.org.

The Society for Human Resource Management is the world's largest HR professional society, representing 285,000 members in more than 165 countries. For nearly seven decades, the Society has been the leading provider of resources serving the needs of HR professionals and advancing the practice of human resource management. SHRM has more than 575 affiliated chapter within the United States and subsidiary offices in China, India, and United Arab Emirates. Please visit us at www.shrm.org.

Interior & Cover Design	Shirley Raybuck
Manager, Creative Services	James McGinnis
Manager, Book Publishing	Matthew Davis
Vice President, Editorial	Tony Lee

Library of Congress Cataloging-in-Publication Data has been applied for and is on file with the Library of Congress.

ISBN (pbk): 978-1-586-44431-0; ISBN (ePDF): 978-1-586-44432-7; ISBN (ePUB): 978-1-856-44433-0; ISBN (eMobi): 978-1-586-44434-1

Printed in the United States of America
FIRST EDITION

PB Printing 10 9 8 7 6 5 4 3 2 1

16-0852 | 61.11508

Table Of Contents

Foreword

Many in the HR profession know and have been affected by Mike Losey. His personal life and professional career have shaped how HR professionals think and act. Now he has written a book on more than HR—on leadership.

Mike challenges HR professionals to be more than good management partners and administrators. He emphasizes the need to create HR leaders and for good HR leaders to create quality leadership throughout their organizations.

Touching People's Lives is a marvelous retrospective journey through this remarkable leader's professional life. Highlighted are lessons learned along the way and implications for not just HR professionals, but also those who aspire to or are required to be leaders.

Since his studies at the University of Michigan; through his work at Ford, Sperry, and Unisys and his role as CEO of the Society for Human Resource Management (SHRM); and through his extensive consulting, he has accumulated stories where leaders touch lives—for better or worse.

His passion for touching people's lives came from an early personal encounter with "Michael," an emotionally disabled young man. From befriending this young man, Mike learned to care about and serve those in need—and later see how such efforts also benefit those who attempt to do the right thing.

His business leadership came from a merger of two computer giants (Burroughs and Sperry) into Unisys, where he learned to attend to and balance people issues in difficult business transitions.

His understanding about the impact of business on personal lives came from observing the chairman of his company struggle as his business career abruptly ended, not only for him but for many others. He learned to have passion for people facing transition.

His recognition of the importance of accurately anticipating the future came from personal experiences in mismanaging needed change, especially racial discrimination and diversity in the workplace.

He also shares how a government's laws and regulations must be clearly understood when changes are proposed—or risk negative impact on more people than an employer could ever touch.

He became passionate about leadership ethics by observing how leaders often give ethics a passing glance in their deliberations. He learned that a strong moral code gives leaders a sense of confidence and consistency.

As president of SHRM, he was unusually successful. Under his tenure, SHRM grew from 40,000 members to greater than 150,000. Loosely coupled HR ideas became grounded in professional requirements.

Look at this career of caring about people, connecting HR to the business, managing diversity, working on competencies, ensuring ethics, and creating a profession! These are the foundations of not only HR but the best of leadership practices today. Some may merely assume that these essential leadership practices just emerged, but through Mike's stories, he shows the evolution of how these ideas became practices.

I have had the privilege of knowing Mike for much of my professional career. He has competence and commitment to advance not only the HR profession but also the best in leadership practices.

His personal journey is the journey most aspiring leadership professionals must take to realize their full potential.

Dave Ulrich, Ph.D.
Rensis Likert Professor at the Ross School of Business, University of Michigan, and partner, The RBL Group

Introduction

I spent far more time trying to write this book than I ever intended. It was start and stop, write and rewrite, and threaten to pitch the whole project, only to come back once again.

First, it was going to be another technical book on the profession of human resource management and its impact, but then I started to feel I had done enough of that.

Then one day it came to me.

I was reading *The Last Lecture* by Randy Pausch with Jeffery Zaslow.

It is a book about a relatively young Carnegie Mellon professor who, as he is dying of pancreatic cancer, is offered the opportunity to lecture one last time prior to his death.

While others might have spent their time between diagnosis and death in other ways, Randy asked himself, "What do I, alone, truly have to offer?"

I thought for myself, "I have my stories."

I have written dozens of articles; given hundreds of speeches; taught more people than I can count; provided expert testimony in complex legal cases; consulted for major corporations, not-for-profits, and government; and been invited multiple times by the U.S. Congress to testify on important pending legislation. In addition, as the Society for Human Resource Management's (SHRM's) president and CEO, I had the opportunity to be engaged in SHRM's professional development programming. This allowed me to meet more than my share of management, educators, and others, many of whom were among the finest leadership speakers and consultants in the world.

As readers, I suspect most of you have had similar experiences.

Someone suggested to me that I might be a little different than just an HR professional, educator, consultant, executive, or speaker. I was fortunate to have had a varied career giving me the opportunity to be all of these, as well as a CEO of a professional society considered to be one of the best in America.

After 50 years in my various roles, I had gained what I consider important perspectives and experiences. Some of these were originally highlighted in speaking engagements or merely in personal discussions. For years, numerous friends and associates have encouraged me to share and preserve my "stories" by writing a different type of book.

If I am to do it, now is the time. When most leaders are at the twilight of their careers (and for me, it is really the "sunset"), they evaluate what was really important and how well they performed in their professional lives.

As these leaders reflect back on their careers, you would think they would highlight what they did to increase the revenue, the profits, the return on investment, and other business metrics for their organizations. However, that is not always true. Frequently, executives recall the many people that they have touched, favorably or unfavorably, by their leadership.

I would hope that they took time to provide advice, mentor, warn, and encourage, and I would also hope they are proud of the actions they took and the decisions they made. Or possibly they now deeply regret that they did not do more of these things.

For the most part, my leadership experiences gave me joy, and they are what encouraged me to write this book.

Thus, this will not be another HR book. Upon years of reflection, I write this book to convey and share examples of leadership successes and failures. People leadership success (PLS) stories are easy to learn from and a way to show others how to effectively lead. People leadership failure (PLF) stories are either a result of a leader's inability to accurately anticipate and plan for important social, economic, market, and other critical changing circumstances, or a result of bad management decisions.

A responsible leader discovers that the impact and actions related to PLFs are much different and more difficult to correct than are failures resulting from a management leadership failure (MLF).

MLFs include quality defects, production shortfalls, missed sales goals, reengineering a design error, or reversing an incorrect accounting entry. These are much easier to correct. For instance, if the finance director discovers that a debit should have been a credit, someone merely reverses the entry—and life goes on.

Dealing with people is much more permanent. With people leadership, those accountable learn that rarely can they go back and make a bad decision a good one. Thus, the people leadership burden is to get it right the first time. There is no greater sorrow if you get it wrong, and you spend the rest of your life worrying about how you negatively affected other peoples' lives—individually or collectively.

The opposite is also true. When a leader favorably touches someone's career or life, there is not only a sense of joy, but frequently the person the leader helped subsequently touches the leader's life in even a greater way.

My one regret is that much of this book will be primarily my experiences and stories. I know there are many such stories with every good leader and other well-intentioned individuals. And for those who cannot think of even one time they touched someone's life in a favorable way, it is not too late.

The greatest joy to me would be hearing your new people leadership success story.

CHAPTER 1

Michael

Throughout my tenure as president and CEO of the Society for Human Resource Management (SHRM), people often asked me how I entered the HR profession. The story is simple. It stems from a college summer-vacation experience I had with Michael, a teenage boy with a cognitive disability.

I had completed my freshman year at the University of Michigan. It was 1958, and I was 19 years old. Summer employment opportunities were bleak.

Then I received a call from Mr. Woodward. In our hometown of Monroe, Michigan, Mr. Woodward was a well-known business executive who worked for the Monroe Auto Equipment Company, now a division of Tenneco, Incorporated. He was the firm's general counsel. I knew him well because, as a teenager, I had caddied for him and his wife at the Monroe Golf and Country Club on numerous occasions.

Mr. Woodward had a special request. One of his three children, Michael, age 14 at the time, was in a special boarding school for children with intellectual disabilities. Michael would be coming home for the summer, and Mr. and Mrs. Woodward needed help caring for their son during the day.

The request was that I arrive at their home at 8:30 each weekday morning to pick up Michael and take him away from the home until Mr. Woodward returned after work. I would be paid one dollar an hour. With no other employment opportunities likely, and with my mother's encouragement (she was a friend of Mrs. Woodward), I became a "babysitter" for a 14-year-old teenager.

I first met Michael when his mother asked me to go to Detroit to pick him up at his boarding school and bring him to Monroe.

I found the school without difficulty. The Woodwards had made previous arrangements to release Michael to me, and, without difficulty, we started on our way home. Almost immediately, I learned that my task was not going to be easy, nor was it always to be a pleasant experience. In the brief 40-some-mile journey to Monroe, Michael tried to jump out of the car several times, thankfully unsuccessfully. I remember thinking, "It's going to be a long summer!"

Finding something to do with Michael each day was difficult, especially since the requirement was that when I arrived at the Woodward home each day, I was to take Michael "away" from his home. Frequently, we would go to my home. However, there was always the challenge of what to do with him and hopefully make his day better.

I had a program for the first day. He told me that he loved baseball and that his favorite position was catcher. Unfortunately, he never had the opportunity to play. We walked down to the sport shop and, with money his mother had provided, purchased a baseball and a catcher's mitt.

We stood the customary distance apart to practice throwing and catching. It was a short experience. On my first throw to him, he put up his mitt only to miss catching the ball and having the ball strike his glasses, breaking the frame.

After that, he did not want to play baseball anymore. However, now we had something to do on the second day . . . go to an optometrist's office and get the glasses fixed. The clerk warned me that it could take a while to repair the glasses. I told her not to worry. Little did she know we now had something to fill that day!

Unbeknownst to me at that time, our experiences together would influence the course of my life forever. And here is how.

On one of those long summer days together, I needed to go to Ann Arbor, where I had to meet briefly with a professor. With that quickly done, I gave Michael a tour of Ann Arbor, showing him where I lived in West Quad at the University of Michigan and other special places around the campus, such as the Diag in the center of campus and the huge football stadium. As we were driving past the university's Museum of Natural History, he asked what it was. I explained, and he asked if they had "any dinosaurs in there."

Always looking for something to do to fill the day, with sometimes pleasing him only a secondary consideration, I remember thinking, "This will be good for a couple of hours."

Michael was immediately drawn to a dinosaur exhibit. I was surprised at his level of interest and knowledge about dinosaurs, and we took advantage of this window of opportunity to spend the remainder of the day at the museum.

Because of Michael's keen and unexpected interest in dinosaurs, the next day back in Monroe, we went to a local hobby shop. I thought, wouldn't it be great if they had a model of a dinosaur, and we could spend a day or two putting it together?

We were lucky. They did have a model of a dinosaur, and from my measly minimum wage, one-dollar-an-hour job, we bought the model. I recall it was all white, with many bones that we had to determine how to assemble. We spent the next two days in my basement, sometimes watching *American Bandstand,* attempting to glue these dinosaur bones together. I tried to have him do as much work as his patience would permit, which was not much.

Intentionally, I had delayed gluing the final piece, which was to go on the long tail. I told him it would be great if he did this himself, thus completing the project. I did not wish to rush him or gawk at him. So, I turned away from Michael and sat in the reclining chair that faced the television.

It was not long before I heard a noise like something being crushed. I thought, "Oh no!" I quickly turned to see what was happening and saw not only Michael's foot crushing the dinosaur into a thousand pieces but also the frustration on his face.

This was the only time I lost my temper with Michael. I did not hit him, but I came close to it. I yelled, swore, and reminded him that we had been working on assembling this model for two days. Then I asked why he had crushed the model with his foot. When there was no answer, I told him I was taking him home, early.

When I arrived at Michael's house the next morning to pick him up, I noted that his father had delayed his departure for work and was waiting for me in the driveway. He wanted to know what had happened the day before. I had already put the incident behind me and told him nothing special had happened.

Then he asked specifically about what happened with the dinosaur. Michael had told his father that he had destroyed the dinosaur. Before I could figure out if I was going to be reprimanded, Michael's father volunteered, "Michael was worried you would not come back today." He continued that Michael wanted to apologize to me for his behavior. Then Michael appeared from the house, as if on cue. He walked directly to me and apologized.

While I was grateful for Michael's apology, I was not totally convinced that his attitude would improve. But it did. From that day forward, Michael's attitude changed. In fact, he improved so much that I was soon able to include Michael in activities with my local college-age friends. No longer did I insist on walking to every place simply because it took more time, which, up until then, seemed like a good way to fill an endless day. On occasion, I would even return in the evening to pick him up and take him with me to play poker with my buddies.

These were important changes. I no longer had a ward but instead a friend.

At the end of the summer, unexpectedly, Michael said that he wanted to talk to me. Michael told me that he did not want to return to the private institution in Detroit. Instead, he said he wanted to attend the local George T. Cantrick Junior High School, the same junior high school that I had attended. He also told me that he wanted to play football there, as I had done.

Remembering his short-lived baseball career and the dinosaur, I warned him that if he went out for the football team, he could not give up as he did so frequently when he got discouraged or frustrated.

However, to my relief and joy, I had witnessed significant changes in his personality and conduct. I observed this in the way he spoke about what he wanted his future to be. The way he talked to me about his desires was with a seriousness I did not know he could apply. His voice was sober. He was obviously wishful for a new life.

Of course, the decision to send Michael to Cantrick Junior High was not a decision I could make, but I spoke with his parents about it, and they supported the idea. This was before the "mainstreaming" of children with special needs became commonplace in public schools. To the parents' credit, they petitioned school officials to admit Michael. The officials said they would give him a reasonable opportunity to prove he could perform satisfactorily, not be disruptive in class, and otherwise be suitable as a regular student.

That fall I returned to my University of Michigan studies, and Michael was admitted to Cantrick Junior High. I hoped so very much that Michael would be able to meet the requirements so that he could remain in the public school system and be treated like any other kid.

A few weeks later, I came home from Ann Arbor for a weekend and was driving past what I hoped was still Michael's school. As I passed the school, I noticed about 40 young boys running around the track in their football uniforms. "My God," I thought, "could Michael not only still be in the school but on the football team? Did he stick it out?"

Then I saw one boy was lagging about 25 yards behind all the others as they ran the laps. Yes, it was Michael.

I honked my car's horn with a small beep to acknowledge that I was there. He looked at me and recognized my car but did not wave or offer any form of recognition. His only response was to put his head down and run like hell to catch up with the other boys. He had made it. He was still there, in school, and on the team. I had touched a life in a very favorable way. Instantly, within me, I felt a joyfulness I had never before experienced. I knew that I had touched his life, but could it be that he had touched mine, too? Yes, and from this experience with Michael, my life has changed forever.

Soon after the beginning of my junior year in college, I discovered that I had an interest in human resources or what was then called industrial relations. I applied for a scholarship in that field. It was a special type of scholarship, reserved for students in industrial relations and was sponsored by RCA Corporation. In addition, it was not just for tuition or books. The scholarship included $100 per month, in cash, for nine months, which could be used on anything.

The scholarship money was especially attractive to me since it would allow me and Annie Liparoto, my girlfriend from the ninth grade at Cantrick, to get married prior to my senior year. Realistically, I had little hope of being chosen for the scholarship. My grades were good, but I worried the grades of others were better than mine. Fortunately, the level of the candidate's maturity was also a criterion for the scholarship. Thinking "nothing ventured, nothing gained," I submitted my application.

Dr. George Odiorne and two other professors in the business school interviewed me for the scholarship. Dr. Odiorne was an influential professor whose research and writings shaped many of the HR policies and practices in the early 1960s.

Dr. Odiorne reviewed my scholarship application and then started the interview by asking me to explain my rather unusual summer job with Michael. I told the story as I have written here, ending in how Michael had succeeded and was still in the public school system. It took a while to tell the story. There were no other questions. Dr. Odiorne spoke for the three-professor interviewing committee when he ended the interviewing, saying, "That will be all, thank you."

I was awarded the scholarship and subsequently began a lifelong relationship with this noted professor. Not only did Dr. Odiorne later hire me to work under his tutelage at the university's Bureau of Industrial Relations; he also encouraged and helped me complete my master's degree. Upon my master's graduation, he recommended me to my very first employer, the Ford Motor Company. A couple of years later, he recommended me again, this time, to Sperry Corporation, where I spent most of my corporate career. Thirty-three years later, when SHRM recruited me to become its president and CEO, Dr. Odiorne provided a final key employment reference for me.

As I write this book, I have often thought of Michael because my experience with him both paved my way into the HR field and encouraged me to work with others to help them reach their full potential. Most of all, I realized how working with Michael that special summer had possibly helped me even more than I helped him.

CHAPTER 2

A Call from the Chairman's Office

The phone rang as it had done too many times that day. I thought, "What is the problem now?"

The executive secretary of the former Burroughs and now new Unisys chairman, Michael Blumenthal, had panic in her voice. Given the difficulties associated with what was the largest computer industry merger up until then, it was not the first time someone had called me in a panicked state. However, a call from the chairman's office was unusual. A panic call from the chairman's office was very, very unusual.

The secretary said an employee had called Mr. Blumenthal's office from his home requesting to speak to him. She asked the employee what he wanted to talk to Mr. Blumenthal about, and he said, "I want him to hear this."

When she asked him what he wanted Mr. Blumenthal to hear, without hesitation, he said, "I have a gun, and I am going to kill myself." The employee's threat was a result of fear related to the possibility of losing his job because of the merger between Burroughs Corporation and Sperry Corporation.

She transferred the employee's call to me. He complained about being under great stress. I assured him that the company could help him with medical intervention and possible counseling and that his supervisor would provide additional support. Fortunately, he did not pull the trigger, and police and other help arrived in time to intervene. He did seek the professional assistance available and was able to return to his job.

That was more than thirty years ago. Even so, when I hear the word "merger," I pray that the executives involved on both sides have very carefully thought through the merit of their merger strategy.

Business schools teach that the first factor of a merger of public companies is to consider the interests of the shareholders. However, in an increasing number of companies, thanks to 401(k) retirement savings programs, the single largest group of shareholders is the corporation's employees. This was the case with the new Unisys.[1]

There are also the interests of suppliers, customers, communities, and—if the organization is big enough—even our nation.

Thus, mergers are great examples of "macro" corporate activities that affect a lot of lives, seen or unseen, especially if the plan does not work out as originally conceived.

Concentrating only on the interests of the shareholders is shortsighted. Yes, shareholders may lose money, but unless they have invested all their assets in a merger that failed, their financial security will not go completely bust. On the other hand, an

---

1   The former Burroughs Corporation practice was to match any employee 401(k) retirement plan contribution with Burroughs stock. Sperry's company match was invested into the investment option(s) the employee had selected.

employee who is also a shareholder can lose both his or her job and investment savings.

Sometimes merger planning can be almost cavalier in terms of considering and attempting to minimize the "people" impact of such strategies. We do much more for wildlife and plants.

The Endangered Species Act (ESA) of 1973 provides important protections for these plants and wildlife. For instance, as of "January 2013, the FWS [United States Field and Wildlife Service] has listed 2,054 species worldwide as endangered or threatened, of which 1,436 (70 percent) are in the United States."[2]

No such protections exist for the millions of good men and women in the world's workforce. Careless business planning and undesirable results are common and unacceptable. Legislation is not the answer. Management representatives must understand and bear the responsibility to do the right thing or live forever regretting their miscalculations and poor decisions. The great universities of the world should not graduate future leaders without the understanding that, when employee issues are involved, you cannot go back and simply reverse your original decision. The damage will have been done. As in my example of the employee's call to Blumenthal, the negative impact on employees may even be severe enough to cause loss of security and self-esteem, as well as depression that could even lead to loss of life.

---

2 https://www.fws.gov/endangered/esa-library/pdf/ESA_basics.pdf

CHAPTER 3

A Case Study (Burroughs and Sperry Merger)

In the mid-1980s, both Sperry and Burroughs had an interest in merging with another company in the computer industry, since they had the same problem. An old Sperry (1910) and an even older Burroughs (1886) were greatly disadvantaged in the computer marketplace by their small market shares. IBM, possessing 73 percent of total market sales at the time, was, by far, the leader in the industry. Sperry and Burroughs had only a small percentage of the market: each at about 3 percent. Leading by such a huge margin, IBM would challenge any potential customers as to why they would ever commit to a new major computer system with smaller computer companies, such as Sperry and Burroughs, and suggest that they were at a greater risk of failing.

Job security at Sperry and Burroughs, especially with longer-serving employees, was of universal concern. As seen in the prior example of the employee attempting suicide as a result of the Sperry and Burroughs merger, an increasing level of stress on the job is frequently a merger consequence.

Regrettably, we were unable to help some other employees manage the fear and stress. I recall one employee who hung himself. Another, a customer service engineer with 25 years of service, when abruptly laid off, went home, got his gun, walked to an empty lot close to his home, and took his own life.

At the time, especially at Sperry, there was widespread concern about the probability of the Burroughs/Sperry merger not being successful. First, the new company quickly renamed itself Unisys, and its merged management had to overcome the growing presumption, substantiated by experience, that most mergers are not successful and do not meet their pre-merger expectations.

In fact, prior to the merger, at its New York City headquarters, Sperry commissioned a major consultant study directed at identifying just what corporation might be the best merger partner for it.

Subsequently, that list was adjusted resulting in a new list of merger candidates that included Amdahl, AT&T, Computer Sciences Corporation (CSR), Cray Research, Cullinet, Ericsson, E-Systems, Harris, Litton, Lockheed, Loral, Martin Marietta, Northern Telecom, NV Philips, Software AG, Tandem Computers, TRW, and even Ford and Chrysler. All companies were evaluated based on the following factors:

- Overall characteristics. Revenue, annual growth rate, market capitalization, current price/earnings (P/E) ratio, specialized markets, recent performance, ownership, and other characteristics.
- Apparent strategy. Examples of pricing strategy, research and development (R&D) investments versus sales ratios, how they compete, cost-reduction efforts, and global strategies.
- Skills. Marketing strengths, research capabilities, service orientation, and standing as a technology leader.

- Why attractive. Skill base and knowledge, technology-driven culture, relative size to add to Sperry's capacity to compete with IBM's world-class standing, complementary markets and/or technology.
- Why not attractive. Loss of Sperry identity, Wall Street perception, basic technology platforms are not compatible, had small market share, profit pressures.
- Attractiveness of Sperry to the merger candidate. Could Sperry's marketing and distribution system and systems-level skills (versus just hardware) interest other organizations to pursue future business in markets where they had a weak presence?

Nowhere was the possible impact the merger would have on employees listed as "minimal" (assuming a little or no overlap of the lines of business, sales, processes, etc.) versus "very similar" operations (in which the greatest impact of the merger would be on elimination of redundant operations and employees.)

Also, conspicuously missing from this favored list of merger candidates was Burroughs—which was ranked in the lowest category as "Not Desirable." The senior Sperry executives' chant was, "There is no way in hell that we should merge with Burroughs."

At the same time, we must assume the Burroughs' executives were going through a similar exercise at their Detroit headquarters. At the top of their list of which company to merge with was apparently Sperry. How could that be?

Burroughs made its initial merger offer to buy Sperry in 1985. The two companies' different opinions on the merit of a merger of Sperry and Burroughs were profound. This is why Sperry management so aggressively resisted the first attempt by Burroughs to merge with Sperry.

SPERRY CORPORATION CANDIDATES FOR MERGER

CATEGORY	DESIRABILITY LEVEL		
	VERY DESIRABLE	MODERATELY DESIRABLE	NOT DESIRABLE
TELECOM	AT&T	PHILLIPS	SIEMENS ERICSSON ITT
IS BULK	AT&T	NCR TANDEM CRAY PHILLIPS NTI	**BURROUGHS** CDG (Boeing) HONEYWELL
SYSTEMS INTEGRATION	MARTIN	TRW - E SYSTEMS LOCKHEED CSC BBN TECHNOLOGIES DBM	PRC LITTON CHRYSLER
IBM	HITACHI	AMDAHL	
MARKETING SKILLS	MARTIN	LOCKHEED CSC TRW	
TECH	HITACHI MARTIN	HARRIS LORAL E SYSTEMS	FORD
SOFTWARE	CULLINET	S/W AG MSA CSC ASK	
IMAGE	AT&T TRW MARTIN NCR	PHILLIPS	

Given the substantial Sperry resistance, Burroughs withdrew its offer, only to return in 1986 with a new and higher offer that an increasingly cautious shareholder-interested Sperry board found difficult to turn down. Burroughs, therefore, acquired Sperry, but only after a long and bitter struggle. In fact, at the final meeting of the two companies' executives, when the negotiations were completed, Mr. Blumenthal went to shake the hand of Gerald Probst, the Sperry chairman, and Probst refused to shake hands.

Yet the companies made an attempt to put a pretty face on the whole thing, calling it a "merger of equals" and providing a new name for the corporation, Unisys.[3] Consulting advice was obtained from merger specialists Mitch Marks and Phil Mervis. Their involvement centered on how to merge the companies correctly and fairly, and their counsel was well intended. Unfortunately, the merger logic was doomed from the start. Those who knew of the Sperry studies and the clear mismatch of a Sperry/Burroughs merger were especially concerned about any merger succeeding.

Executives on both sides understood the inherent and serious challenges facing the newly merged company, forcing many to be concerned with the likelihood of success.

Even so, the new Unisys was setting aggressive goals. The chairman of the new company, Michael Blumenthal, set aggressive objectives. For instance, he suggested that the combined pre-merger revenue of Sperry and Burroughs would double to an annual revenue of $20 billion, with corresponding increases in the price of the new Unisys stock. Led by Mr. Blumenthal, this was the Burroughs management team's macro strategy. The key players— Blumenthal, Paul Sterns, Jim Unruh, and Curt Hessler—knew, or should have known, how any such major plan could affect all shareholders and the company's more than 100,000 employees, as well as their families and their communities. It was critical that the macro strategy be successful, or all of those interests would be negatively affected.

---

3   The name was selected from a contest in which employees submitted ideas for new names. Unisys was suggested not by one but by more than 20 employees. Janet Lehrman, the Burroughs public relations person, headed the renaming effort. The contest rule in the event of duplicate name submissions was that the first entry prevailed. That rule was fair; however, with so many employees coming up with the same name, I suggested we highlight that great minds think along the same channels and therefore give the intended reward to the person who made the first submission, but then give all the other employees who also recommended the Unisys name some type of secondary recognition. Her immediate "no" was one of the first indications of the company's future employee relations challenges.

CHAPTER 4

No Greater Sorrow

Immediately after the merger, the new Unisys Corporation employed more than 125,000 people. Today, after the sale of some divisions and layoffs, Unisys employs fewer than 24,000, an approximately 80 percent reduction in employees.

After the completion of the merger, Mr. Probst (again, the Sperry chairman of the board) was briefly retained as a token representative on the Unisys International Advisory Board but was rarely seen again. The merger activated Mr. Probst's "golden parachute" along with those of others who qualified for this protection after the merger.

Customarily, such contracts are intended not only to insulate and protect executives of a company that may be subject to a takeover, but to retain them during any such struggles. Otherwise, executives of companies "in play" might be tempted to seek other employment for fear they could be disadvantaged in some way, especially if abruptly terminated.

Golden parachutes usually do not become effective until a certain percentage of the company's stock (relatively low, possibly 5 percent) is purchased by another company, presumably one interested in taking over the company. Once the level of qualification is reached, and the executives of the acquired company either lose their jobs or are disadvantaged in sometimes even incidental ways, an executive can "pull the parachute cord," thus figuratively floating to safety, while the rest of the employees may crash.

However, the only executive parachutes activated were for the executives of the acquired company, Sperry. The parachutes of executives of the acquiring company, Burroughs, were not activated because the acquiring company employed them. This difference in treatment between Sperry and Burroughs executives manifested itself in a few different ways. First, Burroughs executives, who were also at risk of losing their jobs in a merger in which "meritocracy"[4] was being advanced, did not have the protection the Sperry executives possessed. This situation proved to be a large hidden pea under the merger agreement mattress.

Furthermore, many of the Sperry executives, especially those approaching retirement, saw the parachute as a gift from the Merger God. They took their money, turned their backs, and simply walked away.

In Mr. Probst's case, at the time of the merger in 1986, he was 63 years old. He previously had committed to relocate, after his retirement, to Salt Lake City. Since the benefit, or payout, from a golden parachute is traditionally 2.99 times the executive's average pay and cost of benefits received for the prior three years, his parachute payout was significant. As a matter of fact, it, was so

---

4   The suggestion was that all management positions in the merged company would be filled on the basis of merit with no preference given to the acquiring company, Burroughs: an excellent objective many would suggest was not met.

large (although dwarfed by today's standards and practices) that the Unisys tax department pleaded with me to call Mr. Probst and ask if his payment, which was due the next day, could be postponed until the tax department could more accurately calculate the amount of the payment. Sarcastically, I asked the department manager if his department could calculate the amount of interest that would be due, for one day, for the multimillion dollar payoff to which Mr. Probst was entitled. They did not think my question was funny, but I had made my point.

I next asked the tax department to estimate, as closely as possible, the amount of the payment required to satisfy Mr. Probst's golden parachute payment. I subsequently contacted Mr. Probst and told him the problem. I asked if it would be satisfactory if we estimated the amount to be paid him and then promptly paid him that amount. The company would then pay any additional amounts, or Mr. Probst would reimburse us, if necessary, when we determined the final entitlement. Mr. Probst immediately agreed. The golden parachute payment was made in that fashion, on time.

As planned, after Mr. Probst left the company, he retired to his new Utah home.

A relatively short time later, in January 1989, I received another telephone call I will never forget. One of Mr. Probst's close personal friends, and a former Sperry employee, called me and asked me to notify other members of management that Mr. Probst had died. Everyone was dumbfounded given the fact that Mr. Probst had been known to be in good health. I suspected a heart attack, but no reason was given or confirmed. The conversations about his unanticipated death were somewhat guarded.

I notified Mr. Blumenthal and other officers. They, too, were all very surprised. I also suggested to Mr. Blumenthal that proper representation from the company should go to Salt Lake City to attend the funeral. Given Mr. Probst's well-known previous disgust with the merger, Mr. Blumenthal agreed that his and other major Burroughs executives' presence would not be appropriate. He instructed me, as a former Sperry executive, to take one of the company aircraft and arrange for suitable individuals to attend the funeral.

I invited former Sperry executives who had previously reported directly to Mr. Probst to join the group. I knew how they related to Probst when they worked for him. I assumed many would feel they owed him some visible respect and appreciation, for it was he who placed these executives in the senior-level positions they had held within Sperry. In addition, we had the convenience of a luxurious executive jet that would allow us to travel from Philadelphia, where most lived, to Salt Lake and back, comfortably, all in one day.

The first executive I called regarding attending the funeral said he had a dentist appointment and did not want to change it. Several others offered equally pitiful excuses. Joe Kroger, the former Sperry president, did attend and traveled independently. Ab Martin, a former Air Force general who also reported to Mr. Probst at the time of the merger, and had previously left the company, reinforced my faith in top management when I saw him sitting quietly in the back of the church. He had made his own personal arrangements to attend the funeral.

So who went on the jet? Rather than come close to begging executives to attend the funeral, I offered seats to those I thought loved and respected Mr. Probst, and his wife, the most: people like his former secretary, administrative services staff, and others—most nonexempt (hourly) individuals. Mrs.

Probst knew all of them well and, I am confident, appreciated their respectful attendance.

Discussions at the funeral fell far short of any type of probing inquiry, but there were subtle hints renewing my concerns about how Mr. Probst may have died.

Later, Mr. Probst's executive death benefit was processed, and his death certificate was submitted to the company. It said Mr. Probst was found dead in his garage in the early-morning hours, on January 15, 1989. The cause of death was later confirmed as carbon-monoxide poisoning and ruled a suicide.

My experience with the Sperry-Burroughs merger started with my helping talk one employee out of suicide; however, I was not able to intervene in other cases, including the suicide of the former Sperry Corporation chairman of the board.

For more than 25 years, I have wondered why Mr. Probst took his own life. Beyond the ever-present uncertainty of why anyone commits suicide, why would such a previously successful executive do this? Did the golden parachute financial resources make no difference to him? What was more important?

It was well known that Mr. Probst felt the merger would never work. He knew and witnessed the initial impact on shareholders, employees, friends, communities, and others. I dreaded to think he felt he had somehow failed the same people or got outmaneuvered. Through this difficult experience, I learned that no one is immune from the personal trauma of major management decisions, which can negatively affect everyone in the organization.

Recalling the wishful post-merger projections of the Burroughs top management, we need merely to compare the results to see how far off a management decision can be. (Since 2010, I have discontinued auditing the Unisys performance.)

	1986	5-Year Plan	2010 Actual
• Revenue	$10B	$20B	$4.6B
• Employees	125,000	Not stated	22,900
• Stock Price	$37	$75	$0.28[1]

[1] Prior to 2009 reverse stock split of 1 share for every 10 shares.

Anything more than characterizing the Sperry-Burroughs merger as a catastrophe would be generous. Regrettably, this is not an isolated occurrence. Other mergers failed to meet expectations and illustrate how touching peoples' lives in such a negative and unfortunate way is almost unbearable. There is no greater sorrow.

CHAPTER 5

Anticipating the Future: The Most Important Part of Management

When William Becker and Paul Greene, two Santa Barbara, California, building contractors, developed a plan to establish motels with rooms at bargain prices, they thought a great name would be Motel 6. This—$6 per night—was the room rate that would allow them to make a profit after covering building and other costs.

Did Bill and Paul believe that their costs would never increase? Did they plan on always charging only $6 per night? What was their planning horizon? A month, six months, a year, a hundred years?

Despite the lack of understanding or even interest in anticipating the future, Motel 6 is now more than 50 years old. It is still Motel 6, but currently has more than 1,100 locations with more than 105,000 rooms in the United States and Canada. Now part of the AccorHotels family, Motel 6 is the largest privately owned and operated hotel chain in North America.

Then too, what about the Burlington Coat Factory? When did it occur to that corporation's leaders that they should sell more than coats?

Had Southwest Airlines' management intended to always serve only the southwestern section of the United States?

What about ENIAC, the world's first computer? When co-inventors J. Presper Eckert and John Mauchly delivered the first computer to the United States government in 1946, what did the inventors think was the potential of this new electronic machine? What impact might their invention have on the future?

I knew Dr. Eckert personally, since he had worked for Sperry while I was there. I loved to talk to him. In one discussion, I asked him how many computers he thought the company would make after its introduction of the ENIAC. His answer was "two or three." As with the rest of the examples, his appraisal proved how difficult it is to accurately anticipate the future—even for the most brilliant people.

However, it is not just the business climate and products and services that are hard to anticipate. Social changes are difficult to recognize and adjust to, also.

For instance, James B. Conant was the president of Harvard University when the G.I. Bill of Rights, formally known as the Servicemen's Readjustment Act of 1944, was originally being advanced in Congress. This act was to offer the 16 million men and women who served in the armed forces during World War II a federal subsidy to continue their schooling or training. The G.I. Bill subsidized tuition, books, and fees, as well as provided a monthly cash allowance for veterans. Qualifying veterans could select the schools they wanted to attend, and the schools maintained control over admission policies.

Most colleges and universities welcomed the prospect of subsidizing students as a way of making up for the under-enrollments of the wartime years. However, Mr. Conant did not see the bill in that way. He worried that the bill would cause a lowering of academic standards. His preference was a bill that would finance education of "a carefully selected number of returned veterans."

Nor did Robert M. Hutchins, chancellor of the University of Chicago, support the G.I. Bill of Rights initiative. In 1944 he wrote an article called "The Threat to American Education." He felt that the G.I. Bill would encourage colleges and universities to lower their standards just to get the federal money. He worried they would not want to reject unqualified veterans or expel those who might fail. He went as far as to predict that colleges and universities would find themselves converted into educational "hobo jungles."

Fortunately, these concerns made no difference in Congress or among the vast majority of other educators. In the fall of 1946, to the surprise of those who had predicted that many veterans were either not suitable candidates for college or would shun higher education after their years on the battlefield, 1,013,000 veterans enrolled in colleges and universities, nearly doubling the nation's college student population.

Government officials and educators consistently underestimated the number of veterans who would use their education benefits.

What was even more surprising than the deluge of veterans on campuses was their academic performance. Far from undermining academic standards, as Hutchins and Conant had feared, the veterans consistently outperformed other students. Many educators also felt that the veterans quickly established a reputation as the hardest-working, best motivated generation ever to pass through the nation's colleges. Some now-famous people may have missed their opportunity to contribute to our society and nation had it not been for the opportunities for continuing education through the GI Bill of Rights.

Among those helped by the G.I. Bill were many famous people, including major figures in public life such as presidents Gerald Ford and George H.W. Bush; Supreme Court justices William Rehnquist, John Paul Stevens, and Byron White; U.S. senators Bob Dole, John Glenn, George Mitchell, Alan Simpson, and Daniel Patrick Moynihan; and U.S. representatives Ronald Dellum and Charles Rangel. Civil rights activists Medgar Evers and Hosea Williams also used the G.I. Bill, as did legendary entertainers Harry Belafonte, Johnny Cash, Clint Eastwood, Paul Newman, and Walter Matthau.[5]

Harvard's president, Mr. Conant, withdrew his earlier criticism and confirmed that the veterans at Harvard were "the most mature and promising students that Harvard has ever had."[6] This proved that even the brightest leaders from organizations with great reputations can be wrong in anticipating the future.

Anticipating the future is the most difficult part of management. Failure to integrate into organizational and strategic planning the impact of changing technology, globalization, customer preferences and needs, manufacturing efficiencies, and other factors would greatly disadvantage any organization. Failure to anticipate changing social issues not only detracts from positive change but too often perpetuates negative impact on people.

An organization's inability to effectively anticipate the future will delay and curtail success, or worse, cause complete organizational failure. When that happens, it not only jeopardizes the

---

5 Suzanne Mettler, "How the G.I. Bill Built the Middle Class and Enhanced Democracy," *Key Findings*, January 2012, https://www.scholarsstrategynetwork.org/sites/default/files/ssn_key_findings_mettler_on_gi_bill.pdf.

6 Diane Ravitch, *The Troubled Crusade: American Education*, 1945-1980 (New York: Basic Books, 1983),

investors' return on investment—or in the not-for-profit world, the fundamental nature of the organization—but also harms employees, usually with greater impact on them than on anyone else.

Equally important is the problem of complacency when the organization appears to meet the requirements of good planning, primarily because it is already very successful in its industry. Unfortunately, more often than not, the organization's need for anticipating the future is often downplayed because of its prior success. Thus an inverse relationship exists: The more successful the organization is, the more the organization needs to accurately anticipate the future. Past favorable performance should not lead organizations into a false sense of security that they are insulated from change. Employers must avoid learning by experience that the taller they stand, the harder they can fall.

Many successful legends in their industries, such as Kodak, Woolworth, AOL, Blockbuster, Yahoo, Blackberry, Pan Am, Sears, and K-Mart risk future tombstones inscribed "Did not anticipate the future." No organization is exempt from the fallout of failing to accurately plan and adapt.

A perfect example of this failure to anticipate the future was an incident I experienced with IBM.

IBM had an excellent reputation not only for its products but also for outstanding employee relations. The foundation of its employee relations practices was a solid commitment to a policy it called "full employment." Even during the realignment of the computer industry in the 1980s, IBM had never laid off an employee.

In addition, the company's compensation and benefits plans were better than those of almost any other company. IBM had a stated compensation policy that it would pay its employees "above the market," a policy that helped ensure that IBM would have highly qualified candidates for employment.

Unisys, however, was responding to the realignments and the requirements to reduce cost within the computer industry primarily by laying off thousands of employees each year.

In addition, Unisys was encouraging employees close to retirement to retire early by giving them an enhanced retirement benefit. However, by industry practices, what Unisys was offering was very conservative.

As a shareholder of IBM, I was aware of the changes it was considering making regarding its financial status. During this time, IBM was beginning to face the requirement to reduce costs, as was Unisys. Soon IBM realized that it had to balance its full-employment policy (no layoffs) with the realization that it had to reduce staff to meet its cost-reduction objectives. This included the closing of selected facilities, a more demanding requirement than merely laying off a small percentage of employees at different locations.

When I learned that IBM was going to close its facilities in Albuquerque, New Mexico, and Boca Raton, Florida, I was anxious to learn how the company would do this. For instance, would it finally start to lay off employees?

Prior to terminating employees, the company did two things. The first was to offer employees at the Albuquerque and Boca Raton sites employment opportunities at other IBM facilities where alternate employment existed. This was a totally satisfactory action. However, in such cases, if employees did not accept a transfer, then they were technically considered resignations, thus protecting IBM's no-layoff reputation.

IBM also created a special benefit for employees with relatively short service, defined as two years or less. If they resigned, therefore, not forcing the company to lay them off, they would be paid two years' pay plus $25,000. Programs such as this were given the name career transition program (CTP), known internally as "Cash to Piss off."[7]

When I learned about this benefit, I was both envious and angry. I was envious given the necessarily much more modest incentives we were providing Unisys employees. I had been conditioned by a different management philosophy. That philosophy was to be fair with employees, keep them informed, and assure them they are being treated and compensated fairly and in accordance with market conditions. In other words, they had the employer's assurance they would be treated about the same as they would be treated at any other employer.

In addition, I had been trained to lead by having good policies and following them. HR was not entitled to more resources than other functions to ensure an effective department. My position was reinforced by Mr. Blumenthal, our new Unisys chairman, when one day when he told me, "You are different than other HR people I know. The others always want to 'throw money off of the balcony' to solve their problems."

As an IBM shareholder, I was angry about the incredibly generous program offered to employees with two years' service or less. I thought they were "throwing money off of the balcony."

I wrote a letter to the chairman of IBM at the time, John Akers. I highlighted that I was a shareholder and appreciated the need for the company to provide reasonable transitional financial assistance to employees who would necessarily have to leave IBM involuntarily or voluntarily through some type of incentive program.

---

7   Jack Schofield, "Obituary: John Akers, the IBM CEO Who Lost the PC Market," *Jack's Blog*, http://www.zdnet.com/article/obituary-john-akers-the-ibm-ceo-who-lost-the-pc-market/.

However, I protested the offer of providing employees of very short service with two years' pay plus $25,000 and described this benefit as "unheard of" and outrageous. For shareholders, it was a terrible premium to pay so that IBM could suggest that these employees left voluntarily and thus maintain its claim of never having laid off an employee.

I argued that these types of payments were more generous than required by law or practice in other companies. This plan was even more generous than European practices, which were generally known as the most demanding and costly termination indemnities.

It did not take long before I received a response from Mr. Akers's "caddy" (a special assistant whom I sarcastically assumed carried Akers's briefcase and wrote letters for him to complaining people like me).

My anger was compounded when Mr. Akers's delegated reply suggested that, once I was an IBM shareholder "for a more significant period of time," I would surely "recognize the importance of IBM's full-employment policy."

I remember thinking, "You will all be handed your heads," and they were.

Subsequently, there was a major downsizing of the IBM workforce. Employment was slashed from 407,000 to 360,000 by the end of 1991.

On January 26, 1993, Mr. Akers was the first IBM chairman ever terminated.

The point is, that had the IBM executives more accurately anticipated the future, they could have taken corrective actions much sooner, including the discontinuation of policies that were no longer suitable for their industry. To so blindly hold to past practice was not only inappropriate but stupid.

CHAPTER 6

Mr. Wynn— Lessons Learned

Anticipating the future is important not only for organizational success but also for a nation's success and
responsibility to its citizens. The failure to anticipate the
future affects many more lives than any one employer.

After two years of great work experience with the
Ford Motor Company, I was recruited in August 1964,
one month after the passage of the Civil Rights Act, to
join what was at the time the Sperry Rand Corporation.

My new employment required me to relocate from
Michigan to Lancaster, Pennsylvania, in the heart of the
Pennsylvania Dutch community. I was to be the personnel
manager of a 500-employee manufacturing plant for New
Holland, a farm equipment company and a fast-growing
successful Sperry division.

One of my first observations was the lack of African-
American employees at my new manufacturing plant in
Lancaster. And when I say, "lack of," I mean none! Nor
were any African-Americans employed at the nearby major
and much larger manufacturing facility in New Holland,
Pennsylvania, the headquarters of the company.

Having come from a highly integrated manufacturing facility with the Ford Motor Company, in the Detroit area, I asked my general manager, Frank Powl, why there were no black employees at our facility or at the larger 2,000-employee New Holland plant. The answer was, "They do not apply."

Not sure what to think about that response and already overwhelmed as a new employee, I accepted his response, thinking, how can a company be accused of not hiring minorities when they do not apply?

However, soon that issue would arise again.

My boss and I received a call from the headquarters office in New Holland informing us that a representative of the U.S. Department of the Navy would visit our Sperry division and, specifically, our plant in Lancaster to review our equal employment opportunity program.

Our parent company, Sperry Corporation, was a major government contractor. Our division, New Holland, manufactured and sold farm equipment. As New Holland, we had not sold a dollar of anything to the United States government, although sometimes I thought we should have been selling them manure spreaders.

Many individuals are now aware of Executive Order 11246, issued by President Johnson, which prohibited federal contractors, and certain federally assisted construction contractors, from discriminating in employment decisions on the basis of race, color, religion, sex, or national origin. Contractors were also required to take affirmative action to ensure that applicants were employed and treated fairly during employment, without regard to their race, color, religion, sex, or national origin. However, this order was not issued until September 24, 1965, thirteen months after I began working at Sperry.

Prior to that, since 1960, a voluntary program for certain government contractors existed and consisted of slightly more than 100 companies. Called the Plans for Progress program, its intent was to encourage covered employers to voluntarily promote full equality of employment opportunities.

The expected visitor, Mr. Wynn, was our assigned Plan for Progress representative.

Mr. Wynn was an African-American man who towered over me. He shared with us that he had worked for the government for many years. He was assigned to the United States Navy to check on the progress of the participating companies in the Plans for Progress program. I felt somewhat intimidated because I was a twenty-five-year-old, first-time personnel manager with the corporation's critical compliance on my own shoulders.

When he arrived, Mr. Wynn went right to the heart of the issue. He asked how many black employees we had on the payroll. I told him none. He asked me why. I gave him the answer I had been given: "They don't apply." He asked, "Why don't they apply?" I was out of answers.

He gently suggested the answer was, "Because you have no black employees on the payroll." The similarity to the chicken/egg metaphor, and which came first, was obvious.

Mr. Wynn continued by informing me that he had been in Lancaster for a couple of weeks and he had heard that our company was an excellent company. He further reported that we paid decent wages, offered a lot of overtime, had excellent benefits, and were otherwise recognized as a good place to work. However, he was also informed by the black community that we did not hire black candidates for employment. Nothing could be further from the truth, I thought. Certainly, we were not intentionally discriminating against

African-Americans. However, given our results, our intentions meant nothing.

He talked about what we might do to improve our situation and overcome the presumption of intentional discrimination. We discussed "affirmative action." He explained it as a necessary voluntary action to overcome the impact of past discrimination. He quoted President Johnson's example, suggesting, "You cannot ask a man who has been forced to carry a ball and chain around his leg for years to merely take the chain off and expect him to run like everybody else."[8]

Also discussed was the concern that even with the changes in the law, African-Americans and other minorities may not immediately respond to new employment opportunities if they felt employer conduct had not changed. He used the term "chilling effect" to describe this situation—a phrase I had never seen in my university textbooks.

He suggested this might be the case in our New Holland facility. Local minorities were possibly discouraged from changing their expectations, such as seeking employment with our company, when they saw no change in our employment practices. Again, this type of situation, he emphasized, would justify what we now know as affirmative action. In other words, special, and hopefully temporary, actions intended to overcome the impact of prior, even unintended, racial discrimination were now needed.

When he left, I was angry. Not at him, but at myself, and even at my former university. Why, I thought, are these concepts

---

8   President Johnson's full quote was: "You do not take a person who, for years, has been hobbled by chains and liberate him, bring him up to the starting line of a race and then say, 'You are free to compete with all the others,' and still justly believe that you have been completely fair. Thus it is not enough just to open the gates of opportunity. All our citizens must have the ability to walk through those gates." http://www.pbs.org/wgbh/amex/eyesontheprize/sources/ps_bakke.html

so simple to understand now, but I had at no time thought of them in that way? In addition, how could I have obtained a master's degree in business, with a major in my chosen field, from the distinguished University of Michigan Business School, and never been taught a single word about civil rights in a business and employment setting?

I remember thinking how critical I had been of the blatant discrimination in the south. How could a bus driver, for instance, make a black person sit in the back of the bus? Then I thought about what my employer and I had permitted to be done, which, in my opinion, was much more serious than where a person sits on the bus. Riding in the back of the bus because of one's color was not fair, was deeply resented and now not permitted, but not getting a good job could have a significant negative impact on one's earning potential and, thus, quality of life forever.

My lack of skill and understanding was embarrassing and shameful. I was negatively touching the lives of people I did not even know and many I would never meet. Worse, I could not go back and make things right. That is when I learned that, with these special social and people issues, management must get it right the first time.

Other issues discussed that day escape me. Looking back, I am confident Mr. Wynn felt he had made his point. He asked if I would be reporting the results of our meeting to the management, and I responded in the affirmative.

The company's management was as eager to know the results of Mr. Wynn's visit as I was to share them. Management hoped to avoid reporting to the corporate office in New York City that the meeting did not go well and that our minor tangential governmental contractor relationship to Sperry would affect the corporation in a negative way.

The top management of the company was surprised at how the meeting with Mr. Wynn had gone, and like me, could not reasonably disagree that Mr. Wynn had a good point that we had not fully considered. At the very least, we could not risk his being correct and ignore his simple explanation for our lack of employment of African-Americans and, to some extent, other minorities and women.

One of New Holland's key officers, and an original owner of the company, Reverend J. Henry Fisher, was also a well-known and respected local Mennonite bishop. With no encouragement from me, or to my knowledge anyone else, Reverend Fisher contacted an unknown number of local African-American church leaders after my meeting with top management. He apologized for any misunderstanding and told the clergy that the company stood ready to work with the black community in an affirmative way to more properly consider African-Americans, and other minorities, for employment. After that, we started attracting African-American candidates for employment, and we started hiring them.

A few months later, Mr. Wynn returned. Expecting his visit, I was very proud of the progress we had made. When Mr. Wynn asked what our minority employment situation was at present, I told him about how African-American candidates had started applying for employment and how we had hired several.

I did not get my expected pat on the back. Instead, Mr. Wynn asked if we gave our applicants for employment any type of paper and pencil test. Attempting to explain our comprehensive testing program, I confirmed that almost all candidates were given a minimum of two tests.

He asked if a specific and well-known provider had designed one of the tests. I acknowledged that was the test we were using. I started to wonder what he was going to teach me this time.

Mr. Wynn asked if he could review a copy of the test we were using. Pointing to a specific question, he asked me, "What does RSVP stand for?"

Without hesitation he said: "Mr. Losey, many of my people are unemployed; they don't have jobs or even hopes for jobs. They do not get printed invitations asking for them to RSVP." Without taking a breath, he continued, "Do they have to know what RSVP stands for to sweep the floor or run a drill press?"

There was no long lecture by Mr. Wynn on why an employment test may not be the best criterion to predict the performance of an employment candidate, especially in the case of minorities. Once again, we were challenged to examine our longstanding practice of testing, possibly unfairly, because of Mr. Wynn's relatively simple but straight-to-the-point questioning.

That day was in 1965, and it was the last day we used that test for those types of jobs.

Many other companies continued to use this type of testing, as well as other questionable employment practices—that is, until Willie Griggs, an African-American, sued Duke Power in the now famous 1971 United States Supreme Court case that carries his name. His complaint was that he had not been adequately considered for promotion. More specifically, he alleged that Duke Power's employment requirements discriminated against him and other minorities like him.

In his case, he applied for a position in one of Duke Power's facilities shoveling coal. He was rejected for failing to meet Duke Power's basic employment conditions. The basic qualifications a person needed to be considered for employment with Duke Power were two-fold. First, the candidate had to pass a general intelligence test. Second, the candidate had to have a high school education or its equivalent.

Surely, the above stated key requirements for a job of shoveling coal could be unreasonable if not absurd. In addition, the question was whether those requirements were reasonable predictors of success on the job. In other words, could Duke Power always conclude that those who did well on tests would always do well on the job and that those who perform poorly on tests would not do well at a given job?

At the Duke trial, the point was made that an African-American candidate for employment or promotion would be much less likely to have achieved a high school education. This was especially true in states like Virginia, where many public schools had been closed, some for as long as five years, denying African-Americans an education. Rather than advancing public school integration, the 1954 *Brown v. Board of Education* Supreme Court decision was so detested by some southern states that they created private schools for white students (called segregation academies). These were unmistakably established in an attempt to avoid the integration of public schools required by the *Brown v. Board of Education* decision. These segregation academies clearly benefited whites and whites only.

As revealed at the trial, some white employees, who had been working at Duke Power for some time, met neither of the requirements of passing the intelligence test or of having graduated from high school and yet performed their jobs as well as those who fulfilled the requirements.[9]

To some extent, Duke Power admitted that the employment requirements may have had a negative impact on minority can-

---

9   Perry Alan Zirkel, Sharon Nalbone Richardson, and Steven Selig Goldberg, *A Digest of Supreme Court Decisions Affecting Education* (Bloomington, IN: Phi Delta Kappa Educational Foundation, 2001), 326. "Griggs v. Duke Power Co.," Wikipedia, http://en.wikipedia.org/wiki/Griggs_v._Duke_Power_Co.#cite _ref-zirkel_3-0.

didates. However, the company argued this was not its intent, and, if the impact was not intentional, the company should not be accused of discrimination and held accountable under Title VII of the Civil Rights Act.

The court disagreed. Someone had to pay for the discrimination impact on individuals that had occurred over the past years. The court felt that, even though management of a given company had not adequately anticipated the negative impact of the high school graduate requirement and the other testing procedures, responsibility for the discrimination should rest with that company, even if unintentional. Unintentional discrimination was now to be considered as disparate impact, which was as unlawful as intentional discrimination.

Fundamentally, the court was saying that the fault was with the management's lack of a reasonable amount of knowledge on discrimination as it would relate to employment policies and practices. Adhering to old practices was no excuse. Duke Power failed to anticipate and plan for much more than just economic and competitive changes. The most important failure was that it neglected the social changes that were occurring in the labor force with its inattention negatively affecting many, many lives. If Duke Power was not to bear this cost, who should? Certainly not the casualty, Willie Griggs?

Was Duke Power the only company that was delinquent in this regard? Far from it.

There were all types of clues that change was coming. For instance, some people think that the first executive order on equal employment opportunity matters was President Johnson's Executive Order 11246. Not the case. It was Executive Order 8802 issued by President Roosevelt in June 1941, prior to the attack on Pearl Harbor. It was designed to prohibit racial discrimination in the national defense industry. It was the first federal action, though not a law, to promote equal employment opportunity and prohibit employment discrimination in the United States.[10]

One of the most ardent advocates for change was J. William Randolph, who led the Brotherhood of Sleeping Car Porters, the first predominantly black labor union.

In a 1940 meeting with President Roosevelt, Mr. Randolph recommended Roosevelt issue an executive order, arguing effectively that black Americans were taxpaying citizens and should have an equal right to employment generated in the defense sector, an opportunity frequently and conspicuously denied by employers. Roosevelt objected, suggesting that such a precedent would be hard to manage and would surely encourage others to also seek preference in employment.

Randolph warned he would be left with no other alternative than to march on Washington. Senator Fiorello La Guardia, who was also in the meeting, then asked Randolph just how many people he thought he could get to come to the nation's capital to protest. His response was several hundred thousand. Randolph got his executive order.

However, when the war was over, the Executive Order was discontinued.

The significance of this event is that when President Roosevelt's Executive Order was discontinued, many companies, in their planning sessions, did not consider that discrimination in the workplace would be an increasingly important issue in the future. How many organizations, absent a requirement, took actions to do voluntarily what others were later forced into doing? Not many.

---

10 "Executive Order 8802," Wikipedia, http://en.wikipedia.org/wiki/Executive_Order_8802.

Discrimination was also prevalent within the United States government sector and especially the United States military. Only one other country, South Africa, fought in World War II with segregated troops. Today many wonder how a United States segregated military could possibly have existed in WWII. How could the government at large, Roosevelt (a respected president), dedicated generals (such as Eisenhower), and scientists (smart enough to build an atomic bomb) not see the inherent unfairness of racial discrimination?

Leaders acted in this way not because they were racist but because, like me in 1964, they lacked the knowledge that only through meaningful diversity and mutual communications and understanding can a fair and harmonious workplace be achieved. And from this, we all benefit.

Even President Lincoln, dedicated to issuing the Emancipation Proclamation, lacked a good understanding of African-American interests. One of his initial remedies to discontinue slavery was to create a country, possibly in Central America, for black Americans. He honestly believed that black Americans would prefer to live in their own country.

When he summoned influential black leaders to the White House for a meeting to discuss his plan, he was disappointed to see their objections.[11] The unanimous response by the leaders was to remind President Lincoln that many black people had been in America before his family and other governmental leaders. The black leaders had no interest whatsoever in leaving what they also considered was their country. What they wanted from Lincoln was change and equality of treatment.

---

11 Kate Masur, "The African American Delegation to Abraham Lincoln: A Reappraisal," *Civil War History* 56, no. 2 (June 2010): 117-144, http://housedivided.dickinson.edu/sites/emancipation/files/2012/07/Masur-article.pdf.

As with Mr. Wynn's short, easy-to-understand, profound suggestions to me, Lincoln's issue of creating a country for black Americans was killed by a fundamental, unequivocal, short, and unexpected, but not debatable, position. For more than one hundred years, the challenge for the United States has been to overcome individual and collective segregation preferences and other forms of racial discrimination by some of its citizens.

The most important effort to end discrimination in the military since World War II was in 1948 when President Truman integrated the United States military by Executive Order 9981—and not by an action of a divided Congress. That same year, he also integrated all federal government jobs under a different order, Executive Order 9980.

Again, how many employers noticed that the largest employer in the United States was making such a dramatic move? How many started to check their own organizations for discrimination and consider how they could more effectively manage and benefit from a diverse workforce? Not many.

In fact, when Truman integrated the military, it was so controversial that two legendary senators, Strom Thurmond from South Carolina and Robert Byrd of West Virginia, vehemently objected.

Senator Thurmond emphasized states' rights and demanded that the "evil forces" in control of the Democratic Party be "cast out." He called Truman's Fair Employment Practices Committee "communistic" and said racial integration of the armed forces was "un-American." He suggested the South must hold the line by stating, "There are not enough troops in the Army to break down segregation and admit the Negro into our homes, our eating places, our swimming pools and our theaters."[12]

---

12 David McCullough, *Truman* (New York: Simon & Schuster, 1992), 667.

Senator Byrd, in 1946, wrote to segregationist Senator Theodore G. Bilbo advancing his post-war beliefs: "I shall never fight in the armed forces with a Negro by my side. ... Rather I should die 1,000 times and see Old Glory trampled in the dirt never to rise again, than to see this beloved land of ours become degraded by race mongrels, a throwback to the blackest specimen from the wilds."[13]

Notwithstanding their leadership talents and intelligence, both men lived to regret their comments and failure to recognize necessary change at a critical time.

Then, in 1954, the United States Supreme Court decided unanimously that earlier Supreme Court decisions on school segregation were no longer applicable. More specifically, education based on "separate but equal access" between races was inherently unequal and thus unconstitutional.

Once again, how many employers, working at their easels in some planning conference room, thought to incorporate into their planning the issue of diversity within the workplace and the changing social and legal requirements? And it is not just the employers. Academics are supposed to prepare students and society for the future. Were they as effective as they should have been? Who helped advance the prediction to expect that if children were going to school together that they would expect to work together?

Just a few years later, the 1957 Civil Rights Act failed to pass as Strom Thurmond filibustered on the Senate floor for 24 hours and 18 minutes against it, a record that still stands. In July 1964, the Civil Rights Act was finally enacted providing protections in accommodations, travel, and, especially, employment.

---

13 "Robert Byrd," Wikipedia, https://en.wikipedia.org/wiki/Robert_Byrd.

As highlighted earlier, I began my job at New Holland in August 1964, one month after the Civil Rights Act became law. The stories that I have shared are illustrative of how poorly I, as a management representative, was prepared. I pledged to myself to do all I could to never allow that to happen again. I would be alert to potential trends and possible future positive strategies.

Fortunately, most citizens' attitudes and employer employment practices changed. I was sure even Strom Thurmond had witnessed that shift and was part of the change, even if delinquently.

About the time I retired, Strom Thurmond was approaching one hundred years old and was still serving as a United States senator. At that age, he was the oldest senator in the history of the United States.

Working in the Washington, D.C., area for more than ten years, I had seen him, generally from afar, and on one occasion testified in front of him at a Senate Labor Subcommittee hearing on the Family and Medical Leave Act. My hidden hope was to find an appropriate opportunity to tell Senator Thurmond how far off he was in predicting the needs and future of our country and its people. Worse, his failure unnecessarily delayed progress, resulting in his touching many peoples' lives in a very negative way.

I so clearly remember seeing him for the last time. My wife and I lived in Mount Vernon, Virginia, and frequently went to a local restaurant called Elsie's Magic Skillet, on U.S. Route 1. Conspicuously, hung on the wall, was an autographed picture of Strom Thurmond, suggesting his regular attendance; although the many times we had eaten there, we had never seen the senator.

However, on one Sunday morning in the spring of 2003, Senator Thurmond arrived at Elsie's along with several associates, presumably staff and others. A couple were African-American. He was brought into the room in his wheelchair and placed close to us. I reminded my wife who he was and how, in my opinion, his outrageous conduct delayed important progress in our nation, especially with the issue of civil rights. I reminded her of his comments when Truman integrated the military and, subsequently, how he ran for president on a segregationist platform, how he changed from a Democrat to a Republican, and how he had represented South Carolina forever, it seemed, regardless of his conduct and age.

He was preparing to leave the Senate as he approached his hundredth birthday. And I knew he was getting ready to return to South Carolina. As we were leaving the restaurant, I thought this was my chance to finally express my disappointment about how he surely held up the civil rights progress in our nation. I stood up, turned toward him and noticed he was looking straight into my eyes. He instinctively knew that I recognized him. He said nothing as he merely nodded his head as to confirm it was him. I must admit, the dynamics of the situation "choked me up." All I could utter was, "Have a safe journey back to South Carolina, Senator." I walked out of the restaurant with a lump in my throat and small tears I tried to hide.

A month later, in June 2003, soon after he returned to his beloved state of South Carolina, he died.

CHAPTER 7

Touching People's Lives—More Learning

Social and economic changes are evolving events. They may not be predictable. Recognizing social and economic changes is not like turning on the light switch and everyone suddenly seeing and understanding everything. From a leadership perspective, the earlier that change is detected, the better the leadership. Even more importantly, once change is noted, it is necessary to determine how past practices will be affected and to take the right course of action in the future. Just anticipating change is not enough.

"I have never had a woman complain about sexual harassment."
—MIKE LOSEY, MID-1970S.[14]

When I was in my early thirties, I was promoted to the top HR job within the New Holland division of Sperry. It was the position I was shooting for and overjoyed when I got it. The New York corporate office also told me that

---

14 This chapter is dedicated to the late Peggy Singley.

I was the youngest Sperry vice president in the history of the company.

In retrospect, I now wish they had not told me that, because I believe the promotion, and the related comments, contributed to my getting a very "big head." After all, I had been with the company about ten years and had a total working career of only two more years. Then one day, in my self-elevated state and while talking to my secretary, Peggy Singley, I made one of my pronouncements. With mounting self-proclaimed confidence, I had examined an issue and had something profound to say about it.

The issue was sexual harassment.

In the mid-1970s, this subject was gaining a lot of attention, so much attention, in fact, that my questioning contention was: "I have been in HR all these years and never once have I had a woman complain to me about sexual harassment."

Peggy did not respond, other than looking at me in an eyebrow-raised curious fashion she had never done before.

She left my office, and about fifteen minutes later, she returned with the general counsel's secretary and the president's secretary. They shut the door. Peggy suggested that, because they thought so much of me, they could not allow me to remain so uninformed about women and sexual harassment. This was especially true given my responsibility for avoiding any kind of harassment or discrimination in our workforce. They wanted to "set me straight."

Each woman reflected on the sexual harassment she had experienced in her working career. Simply stated, I was dumbfounded. I knew these women very, very well. I had no idea they had been subjected to harassment, or worse, the likelihood that many others had experienced a similar fate. There was no way I could challenge them, given their sincere and vivid recollections.

That night I discussed the sexual harassment issue with my wife. I explained how I was so unprepared for the comments of these women. Admitting that it was likely I was out of touch with the reality of a woman's world, I asked my wife, when she had worked, what had she experienced?

She responded that she was not the least bit surprised at what the women had shared with me. She immediately verified that similar incidents had happened to her. In our more than fifteen years of marriage at the time, we had never previously discussed this issue. Now that I had brought the subject up—and she too recognized my uninformed status—she told me about several workplace incidents that ranged from being merely irritating to a concern for her own safety.

What was the problem? In part it may have been because all of our key division heads and managers were men. It was as if the women lived on a different planet. We had no meaningful diversity, the cornerstone of universal sharing and understanding. We had seen it previously with our issues of not fully understanding the perspectives of local African-Americans in our company.

Again, now looking backward, with improved insight, given the women's growing participation in the workforce throughout the 1960s and 1970s, we likely failed to recognize the situation as being as important as it was going to become.

The Equal Employment Opportunity Commission (EEOC) reinforced the growing interest in preventing, and helped explain, sexual harassment in 1980. The EEOC issued regulations defining sexual harassment and stating that it was a form of sex discrimination prohibited by the Civil Rights Act of 1964. The major Supreme Court 1986 case of *Meritor Savings Bank v. Vinson* confirmed that "sexual harassment" was a violation of Title VII, notwithstanding the lack of specific reference to sexual harassment in the act. The court established the standards for analyzing whether the conduct was unwelcome and levels of employer liability, and said that speech or conduct in itself can create a "hostile environment."[15]

Leaders who touch peoples' lives need to pause and question just how much they really know about not only economic but social issues within the workplace. If such a major issue as sexual harassment can stay under the radar not only for the general management, but also for an HR person charged with promoting understanding and communications, what are the implications? How do we know when management knows enough to manage? How can decisions be good ones when there is a lack of diversity and effective two-way communications between leaders and those they lead?

The problem of leaders, especially executives, "staying in touch" with workplace issues is that an inverse relationship exists. The higher the executive goes, the less likely he or she will be able to stay in touch, unless special efforts are made to do so. A good first step would be to include in the organization's strategic plan not only the usual economic, technological, regulatory, product, competitive, and other conditions, but also a section dedicated to potential social and employee relations issues and the need for possible changes.

Freddie

In 1965, I was informed that our old New Holland Civil War-era Lancaster plant would be closed. We would move all

---

15 "Sexual Harassment in the U.S. Workplace," Wikipedia, https://en.wikipedia.org/wiki/Sexual_harassment_in_the_US_workplace.

operations from the eastern part of the United States to the Midwest where we would not only be able to expand but be closer to many of our U.S. farm equipment dealers.

The chosen site was Grand Island, Nebraska. Although the third-largest city in Nebraska, it was a relatively small town with a modest labor force. In addition, the labor market was very competitive because we were in the midst of the Vietnam War. As a result of the war, the government reopened the Cornhusker Army Ammunition production facility that had sat idle since the Korean War. This major government contractor would be hiring many more employees than we would be hiring and would have the advantage of much greater government contractor wage scales. Also, Swift & Company was building a brand new meat processing plant in Grand Island and would be in operation before we were.

Again, given our special link to Sperry Corporation, a major defense contractor, we had to ensure that we did the best job possible in terms of recruiting minorities.

One Saturday morning we were testing some candidates for clerical, administrative, and technical positions. We had a full room. While giving these candidates the instructions for the test, I noted that one of the individuals was an African-American man.

The testing began. The test was designed so most people would not have enough time to finish it. However, before the time was up, the African-American laid down his pencil, giving me the impression that he had given up on the test.

Grand Island and the surrounding area had a very small percentage of African-Americans and other minorities in what we would consider the local labor market. We had already recognized that special actions would be required to hire our share of those candidates. Therefore, my first reaction to seeing this African-American candidate's action was, "Nuts! Why is he giving up?"

My interest in him grew greatly when I discovered he had *not* given up on the test. He was the first person I had ever seen complete the test in the allotted time. I encouraged him to consider our company; however, Swift was hiring also, and that was where he decided to work and where he subsequently served as a supervisor.

I had fallen into another trap in spite of how much I had learned previously. If a white candidate had laid down his or her pencil before the allotted time had expired, would I have assumed the white candidate was giving up on the test? Probably not! My initial judgment about this black man having given up was a terrible mistake caused by my inequitable assumptions. I was chagrined and mutely embarrassed as I thought of my now faraway Mr. Wynn. I had let down two people, Freddie and Mr. Wynn.

Tonto

About the same time, we had another African-American candidate apply for work. His name was Tonto, and he was a young man interested in a position in our machining department. Given the infrequency of minority candidates, when he walked into our employment office, my staff immediately alerted me.

He interviewed well, and we offered him a job. He accepted. When he reported for work on his first day, I counseled him on what to expect in terms of the nature of the work and related requirements. However, in Tonto's case, I added one additional element.

I informed him that he would be the first African-American employee at Grand Island's New Holland site. I told him I was confident there would be no special issues related to his race; however, if he was confronted with any such problems, he should notify his supervisor, who would immediately notify me.

Tonto worked one night and did not return. I was worried that something had happened, so I called him at home to follow up. The only explanation he offered was that there were some family issues involved. I reminded him that the company had a "three-day quit" policy. In other words, if he did not report within three days with a satisfactory reason for his absence, he would be terminated.

He never got back to the company. He was terminated.

Several months later, I was at a meeting, sponsored by the Grand Island Chamber of Commerce, on the issue of equal employment opportunity. Many employers had been invited as well as a number of influential African-American community leaders, one of whom was Mr. Washington.

Mr. Washington raised his hand to ask a question. He directed his question to me and asked, "Mr. Losey, how many African-Americans does New Holland employ at your factory here in Grand Island?"

My response was that at the present time, we had no African-Americans on the payroll; however, I gratuitously added that we had hired one African-American man (Tonto), but he had quit for personal reasons.

Mr. Washington responded loud enough for all to hear, "Mr. Losey, do you know why Tonto quit?" Apparently, he knew all about Tonto (I had not mentioned Tonto's name). Not waiting for me to reply, he followed with, "He didn't want to be Jackie Robinson!" The room went quiet.

How stupid could I have been, again? Mr. Washington needed to say nothing more. It came to me! Isn't starting a new job difficult enough for anyone? Why did I need to put the extra burden on Tonto? What was I telling him? Never make a mistake, never miss a day of work, because that would reflect poorly on his race and could disadvantage future African-American candidates. I felt the recurrence of sorrow because I had once again touched someone's life very negatively.

I never saw Tonto again. However, almost 50 years later, I still recall what I did and regret it. From a distance, I followed Tonto's progress through others, quietly. I found out that he continued to live in Nebraska and subsequently opened a business and did well.

Audrey

Audrey was the wife of Freddie, the candidate who finished the pre-employment test early and subsequently went to work with the Swift Company.

In our continued search for African-American candidates, I was told about Audrey. She was a graduate of Hastings College, was popular in her church choir, well liked, and not currently working.

I was looking for an administrative assistant and called her. I informed her of the position availability and asked if she might be interested. She asked if I was serious, and I responded, "Of course."

Then she told me how she had applied for a job with a national department store chain in Grand Island but was told by the store manager (whom she knew) that he would not be able to hire her. He volunteered a response that he had a concern about how the customers would react to his hiring a black person for a sales position. Deplorably, this obvious intentional discrimination was conducted by a national department store chain even after the passage of the 1964 Civil Rights Act.

I convinced her that our company's and my personal interest in recruiting her was sincere, and she agreed to an interview. I hired her shortly thereafter. She was an excellent employee and worked for New Holland until she retired many, many years later.

No sorrow here. Knowing Audrey and what she has accomplished has been a joy.

The African-American Field Service Representative

A field service representative was a New Holland employee in the sales and service group that worked with dealers and major customers. Field service representatives were expected to provide certain training and otherwise assist the dealers and customers with service-related problems.

In the early 1970s, we were recruiting for field service representatives with an expanded effort of recruiting at predominantly African-American colleges and universities. Fortunately, we found a good candidate with a sincere interest in working for us. He was from the South and had a keen interest in working in the southeastern part of the United States.

Soon, some dealers learned that an African-American field service representative might be assigned to their territory. They apparently made a "suggestion" to our branch manager that it would be better for this young man to work in the North where he would be better accepted.

That recommendation worked its way up the system directly to the North American vice president for marketing and sales. He called me to talk about changing this candidate's territory to somewhere in the North.

Usually, staff people, like me, attempt to assist and influence line management but also recognize that the line management generally has the final say. In this case, I could not permit changing the candidate's offer to work in the South. To permit the dealers to constructively veto our employee's assignment, because of his race, would not only violate the law but be inherently unfair.

My colleague pushed back, suggesting, as anticipated, that he was responsible for the ultimate decision on job assignments in his division, not me. I reminded him that we both reported to the president of the company. We shared an interest in doing the right thing, I suggested. Then I advised that he and I needed to work together to ensure that we did not allow our shared boss to make a mistake. I proposed we "meet at the corner office" (the president's office) and be ready to present our respective positions thus facilitating a quick decision by the president.

At that point, to my surprise, he suggested that going to the president's office was not necessary. Furthermore, he let his territory managers know that if a dealer refused to accept one of our field representatives because of race, that the dealer had better be ready to hand in his or her franchise.

Thereafter, we had no problems. In fact, having an African-American field service representative produced some unanticipated benefits. African-American farmer lived in the area. Other competitor dealers lacked African-American field service representatives. Soon, those African-American farmers learned of and welcomed our African-American field representative, gaining additional business for the local dealer. Yes, we were learning, slowly getting better.

CHAPTER 8

Government Touching People's Lives

When we consider touching people's lives, all the employers in a country cannot come close to affecting the lives of the country's citizens as much as national government. Therefore, if we are serious about positively touching people's lives, simply attempting to influence practices at work is not enough.

Individual citizens in the current democracy models around the world have the opportunity to participate in their democracy. Participation ranges greatly from being president of their nation to the citizen who votes only occasionally, or worse, is completely indifferent.

Most organizations recognize their business interests within their country's democratic system, includes making sure that they are aware of changes in government rules and regulations. In other words, corporate taxes, legislation that may affect the cost of doing business, and the implementation of certain rules and regulations must be carefully thought out and understood.

Frequently, the people best suited to provide input to government leaders are already in government service, business, or the not-for-profit world. Unless those who possess special qualifications and experience actively participate in auditing, reviewing, and proactively providing input, a nation's government is substantially disadvantaged.

FMLA: We Did Not Have This Problem in the States That Have This Type of Law

When Bill Clinton became president of the United States, one of his top priorities was to create legislation providing protection and specific benefits for employees who needed some type of family or medical leave.

The Family and Medical Leave Act (FMLA), as subsequently established, entitled eligible employees to take unpaid, job-protected leave for specified family and medical reasons.

Both the House of Representatives and Senate were seeking testimony on this subject from, for instance, Secretary of Labor Robert Reich and other U.S. Department of Labor (DOL) representatives.

I was also invited to testify on this subject before the U.S. Senate Labor Subcommittee. Of the several people testifying that day in 1993, I was the last to comment on the proposed FMLA. All the others had spoken favorably about the act and suggested no changes to what was being proposed.

In my capacity as SHRM's CEO, I was asked to testify on the proposed legislation from an employer's viewpoint.

Recognizing the interest in this bill and the high level of support for it, I limited my testimony to commenting on how this legislation might actually work, if enacted. After all, our SHRM members would be the ones who would have to implement this new law.[16]

The first issue was how to integrate the requirements enacted by the Fair Labor Standards Act of 1938 with the proposed FMLA. For instance, under the proposed FMLA legislation, qualifying employers would have to provide for intermittent leave. Intermittent leave occurs when an employee does not take a full day of absence for family or medical leave purposes. However, the employer was not required to compensate the employee for the time taken for such purposes.

I suggested that the scenario was not a problem for nonexempt employees;[17] however, it would be a problem for exempt employees. This was because an existing long-standing DOL policy did not allow for exempt employees to be "docked" for absences of less than one day. If an exempt employee was docked, for instance, for taking two hours off for a doctor's appointment, under the existing guidelines, the employer might need to change the exempt employee's status to nonexempt. That change could disadvantage the company by requiring overtime payments for highly paid individuals. The original wage and hour legislation had always presumed greater work hour flexibility for "salaried" employees. For instance, salaried exempt workers may need to work more hours one day or one week than another. Logic follows that an exempt employee who is ineligible for overtime payments should be entitled to reasonable time off, during any working day, and should not be docked for that time off.

---

16 A complete C-SPAN video on this hearing can be found at http://www.c-span.org/video/?37338-1/family-medical-leave-legislation. Mr. Losey's testimony begins at 1:48:00.

17 There are two classes of employees for purposes of administration of wage and hour law: nonexempt and exempt. Nonexempt simply means the employees are not exempted from the law and will benefit from all provisions of the law, such as overtime payments. Exempt means that they are exempted from many of the provisions of the law, especially overtime payments.

I began my testimony by reviewing this contradiction and highlighting that if not changed, the proposed bill would require employers to pay their exempt employees for incidental, less-than-a-day FMLA absences, but not pay the nonexempt employees.

Senator Ted Kennedy understood the problem and turned to Secretary of Labor Reich asking, "Bob, can you fix that?"

There was a brief interruption while Secretary Reich turned to his staff sitting behind his seat and consulted with them.

Apparently, this contradiction had not been anticipated. However, very quickly, Secretary Reich responded to Senator Kennedy with a simple "Yes!" The result: Employers would not be required to compensate employees, including exempt employees, for FMLA absences of less than one day without violating the exempt "no docking" rule; however, they could pay for the exempt staff member absence if they preferred to do so.

The next topic during my testimony was how the FMLA leave provisions would be integrated with the existing COBRA law.[18] COBRA requires employers that were providing health insurance to their employees to continue providing the insurance for up to eighteen months of coverage beyond the employee's termination date. The cost of that coverage is whatever the company's cost was for such insurance, but paid totally by the employee.[19]

Under the proposed legislation, eligible employees would be able to take up to twelve workweeks (three months) of nonpaid leave in a twelve-month period for one or more of the qualifying reasons. During that period, employers would also be required to continue group health insurance coverage for an

18 COBRA is a health continuation law that received its common name from the congressional budget bill that it was added into, named the Consolidated Omnibus Budget Reconciliation Act.

19 Plus 2 percent for administrative charges, if the employer elects to apply such cost.

employee on FMLA leave under the same terms and conditions as if the employee had not taken the leave. If, for instance, the employer was paying 80 percent of the health insurance cost and the employee 20 percent, unlike COBRA, the employer would continue to pay the 80 percent of the cost.

The question I raised to the committee was what happens when the employee's twelve-week FMLA leave ends? Of course, if the employee returns to work, the FMLA has served as intended, that is, the employee gets his or her leave and is reinstated without loss of pay or benefits, and the employer retains, presumably, a good employee.

However, what happens if the employee does not return to work and instead quits after taking the leave? In terms of the COBRA benefit that kicks in at termination, how many months of continued insurance eligibility does the individual have? Does the employee have eighteen months as prescribed by COBRA or eighteen months minus the three months the company has already provided by the FMLA requirement to continue insurance as though employed?

Senator Chris Dodd, chair of this Labor Subcommittee, reacted quickly. Apparently neither the bill's proponents nor the DOL had anticipated this question. Raising his voice, he challenged me and noted that many states already had a family and medical leave program for employees and that he had studied this type of legislation for many years and never once heard of this issue.

He was basically asking why I was bringing up this issue now. He kept suggesting that if what I was talking about was a serious problem, then why had it not shown up in those states that had family and medical leave laws already. He, and Senator Kennedy, both suggested I was exaggerating an issue they had not even heard of, notwithstanding their substantial and long-standing experience with this type of legislation in some states.

It was obvious the senators did not realize that those states that already had FMLA laws did not include the requirement of health insurance continuation. One state had attempted to do so, but the U.S. Supreme Court held that the state FMLA law would violate the Employee Retirement Income Security Act otherwise known as ERISA.[20]

When Senator Dodd continued to challenge me, I finally had to inform him how no state had created a family and medical leave law requiring the continuation of employer health insurance as was now being proposed in the federal legislation. Therefore, there was no experience with this untested government-sponsored requirement that qualifying employers had to provide this benefit. Clearly, the federal government was establishing a new employer requirement and employee benefit.

Senator Dodd abruptly turned to his staff seated behind him and asked, "Is that true?" Although not publicly announced in the hearing room, my point was confirmed, since we moved on rapidly without continued debate on that subject.

My recommendation was to change the proposed law in the event that an employee, in anticipation of quitting his or her job permanently, would use the FMLA to obtain three months of employer-sponsored health insurance coverage while never intending to return from the leave.

I proposed that when the FMLA-provided twelve weeks expired, the remaining COBRA benefits would be reduced by

---

20 In the event multistate employers would wish to extend health care benefits to, for instance, all United States employees in all states, the ERISA preemption does not allow individual states to pass their own employment-related health care laws. Such laws in possibly 50 states would severely complicate the establishment and administration of such employer-sponsored plans nationwide.

the twelve weeks the employer had already sponsored, leaving the remaining COBRA entitlement at fifteen months and not eighteen.

Senator Kennedy came to Dodd's rescue by suggesting COBRA is not really a meaningful benefit since many employees cannot afford to pay the total cost of the insurance. I highlighted that the actual cost for the employer was even greater for someone on COBRA than on its normal insurance coverage. This is because the people who are likely to elect COBRA are those who know they will use it. Therefore, the experience rating and the actual employer cost could be as much as 150 percent more than the employer's cost for other employees.

In addition, given Senator Kennedy's concern about the very expensive cost to employees for COBRA, I suggested to Senator Kennedy that he had just confirmed my concern that terminated workers may attempt to use the proposed Family and Medical Leave Act and its mandated benefits and not COBRA.

Logic made no difference. My suggestion died. Now, employees who go on FMLA in anticipation of quitting, and then go on COBRA, receive twenty-one months of employer health insurance eligibility, whereas a regular employee who gets laid off receives only eighteen months of coverage.

CHAPTER 9

The U.S. Congress and the Laws It Passed But Did Not Follow

The Family and Medical Leave Act (FMLA) was also being considered by the House of Representatives. Again, I testified on behalf of the Society for Human Resource Management (SHRM), providing essentially the same testimony I gave in the Senate.

During my testimony, I stressed to the House leaders how important it was for everyone, including their staffs, to understand the nuances of this and other laws that affected our workforce. However, the chairman of the committee highlighted that the employees working in the Senate and House of Representatives, the legislative branch of our government, would not be covered by this new legislation. I was reminded that Congress had historically excluded itself from all legislation that risked enforcement by the executive branch of our government. As just one example, to include Congress in the FMLA, would, by its interpretation, allow the executive branch of the government to enforce, or otherwise interfere with, the actions of the legislative branch, thereby violating the U.S. Constitution's separation of powers requirement between the executive and legislative branches of our government.

After the hearings, I asked my vice president for government affairs, Sue Meisinger, about this situation. She confirmed that employees in the House and Senate did not have the protections of even the most basic of our nation's labor laws, such as overtime pay, equal employment opportunity, disability accommodations, or even legislation related to employee safety on the job.

My sarcastic, immediate response was this explains how some of these laws get passed, yet have issues, because those advancing these laws do not have to abide by the laws they pass. Sue not only agreed but confirmed that this issue had been on SHRM's legislative affairs priority list for some time.

I encouraged Sue and her director of congressional affairs, Deanna Gelak,[21] to redouble their efforts and to do whatever was necessary to change this practice that shielded the legislative branch of the United States government from the real world.

They loved my support and, from then on, SHRM took the lead in gaining the support of other companies; employer associations; and civil rights, labor, and additional associations that were also concerned about this practice. Coordinating actions through the national Congressional Coverage Coalition, which Ms. Gelak chaired, made progress to promote these important changes.

Many knew that congressional leaders had for years blocked prior proposed changes in applying labor laws to their staffs. Our hope was that Congress would not be anxious to admit to and have to defend this exclusionary practice with such weak justification, regardless of how old the tradition was.

---

21 Deanna Gelak, President, Working for the Future, LLC, and congressional expert, contributed to this chapter.

The group's proposal to change these laws for the Senate and House were accepted and translated to legislative bills that were introduced on January 4, 1995. With new momentum from Representatives Newt Gingrich and Dick Armey's Contract with America,[22] the Senate and House acted quickly, passing the new law January 17, 1995. President Clinton signed the bill only six days later. Therefore, in less than three weeks, an ancient tradition was reversed—and reversed dramatically. For instance, in the House of Representatives, the vote was 390 to zero, and in the Senate, 98 to 1. The sole "no" vote was from the longest-serving senator at the time, and one who was steeped in tradition, West Virginia's Senator Robert Byrd.

The Congressional Accountability Act of 1995 (CAA) became the first piece of legislation passed by the 104th United States Congress.

The law requires Congress to follow many of the same employment and workplace safety laws that apply to business and the federal government. The act also established a dispute resolution procedure as an alternative to filing claims in federal court. The act is administered and enforced by the United States Congress Office of Compliance.

Specific Laws Applied

The CAA originally applied twelve specific laws to the U.S. Congress and its associated agencies, giving various rights to the 30,000 employees in the legislative branch:

- The Americans with Disabilities Act (ADA). The legislative branch must make its public services, programs, activities,

---

22 "Contract with America," Wikipedia, https://en.wikipedia.org/wiki/Contract_with_America.

and places of public accommodation accessible to people who have a disability.

- The Age Discrimination in Employment Act of 1967. Employees age 40 or older cannot be discriminated against in personnel actions because of their age.

- The Federal Service Labor-Management Relations Statute. Certain legislative branch employees have the right to join a union and collectively bargain with an employing office.

- The Rehabilitation Act of 1973. Employees cannot be discriminated against in personnel actions because of a disability, and offices may be required to accommodate the special needs of a person with a disability.

- Title VII of the Civil Rights Act of 1964. Employees cannot be harassed or discriminated against in personnel actions because of race, color, religion, sex, or national origin.

- The Fair Labor Standards Act of 1938 (FLSA). Employees must be paid at least the current minimum wage, and certain employees not exempted from the Act are entitled to overtime pay.

- The Family and Medical Leave Act of 1993. Employees are entitled to twelve weeks of leave from work for certain family and medical reasons.

- The Worker Adjustment and Retraining Notification Act of 1989. Employees are entitled to be given advanced notice of an office closing or mass layoff.

- The Occupational Safety and Health Act of 1970. Workplaces in the legislative branch must be free of hazards that are likely to cause death or serious injury.

- The Employee Polygraph Protection Act of 1988. With limited exceptions, employees cannot be required to take a polygraph (lie detector) test.

- The veterans' employment and reemployment rights in Chapter 43 of Title 38 of the United States Code and amended in 1998 to include portions of the Veterans Employment Opportunities Act of 1998. Employees cannot be discriminated against for past or present duty in the uniformed services, and those who leave work to perform uniform service are entitled to be reemployed in their old job after a service obligation ends.

Witnessing the Benefit

Given SHRM's and my personal involvement in advancing this new law, congressional officials subsequently asked me to provide training to the staffs that would be responsible for administrating this brand-new law in Congress.

On the appointed day, several hundred people were at the training program held at the Longworth House Office Building. We started with one of the most basic and longest-standing laws, the FLSA.

Because the legislative branch employees had previously been excluded from this law, they were generally not paid overtime, and their superiors did not have to worry about how many hours their employees worked. The new law would change this practice, since accurate records of time worked by nonexempt employees is a fundamental requirement of the FLSA.

A hand went up in the audience. It was not for a question but instead for a statement. The individual said, "We can't keep records of the time employees work because we don't have time cards." My answer was that "you do not need time cards, or clocks as such. However, you will need an accurate record of all time worked for anyone eligible for overtime payments. If you do not have a system to keep such records now, you will have to create one."

Another hand went up. Again, another statement rather than a question. The person blurted out, "We cannot pay overtime. It's not in the budget!" My answer was quick and direct. "It makes no difference. This is now the law. You have to follow the law."

I had a smile in my body someplace but not on my face—to hide my joy. Yes, one of the benefits of this new law would be that senators, representatives, and their staffs would certainly better understand the impact of the labor laws they pass in the future.

Where Do We Go from Here?

Congress has implemented many changes as a result of the CAA. It has identified more than 27,000 workplace hazards through health and safety inspections and has made the Capitol complex more accessible for people with disabilities. However, it still has much work to do to meet the intent behind the legislation.

For instance, as of the date of this writing, Congress has exempted itself from "Obamacare" (the Patient Protection and Affordable Care Act) enacted on March 23, 2010, as Public Law 111-148. Moreover, Congress has not instituted a mandatory requirement to post employee rights, does not have whistle-blower protection, and has failed to implement regulations for several CAA laws that apply to the private sector. For example, although Congress has conducted disability accommodations reviews and made much progress in this area, they have not implemented regulations for the ADA, and their Office of Compliance is waiting on Congress itself to pass its own regulations.[23]

---

23 Congressional Office of Compliance, *FY2015 Annual Report: State of the Congressional Workplace*, http://compliance.gov/sites/default/files/FY2015%20Annual%20Report.pdf. The report recommends a requirement for posting notices of congressional workplace laws and whistle-blower protections.

Also, the U.S. Department of Labor issued new overtime regulations to "modernize and streamline" the FLSA for the private sector on May 17, 2016,[24] to be effective for the private sector on December 1, 2016. However, Congress is still using the outdated FLSA regulations from 1996 for itself. In that year, the salary levels were only $155 for the administrative exemption and $170 for the professional exemption. So despite the enactment of the CAA, for the past twelve years, Congress has not yet fully followed the FLSA.

What is so important to recognize is that the implementing regulations, especially for employment laws, contain all the specific compliance requirements and are often the main crux of a law. Not promptly developing such regulations runs the risk of falling short of the original CAA objective—to parallel the requirements and protections inherent in our nation's long-standing labor laws.

Indeed, one might wonder if selective coverage of statutes, without the full compliance of current implementing regulations, might actually provide lawmakers with a false sense of security that they understand our nation's labor laws.

Although the enactment of the CAA has accomplished much good, Congress should review the effectiveness of its own attempts to provide congressional employees labor law consistency. It went to the effort to create a separate enforcement agency in the Office of Compliance, so it needs to truly allow it to function. Is it not time for Congress to adequately empower the Congressional Office of Compliance, that it took pains to create, and to comply with our nation's labor laws alongside the private sector?

---

24 http://www.littler.com/president-obama-directs-department-labor-revise-federal-overtime-regulations.

CHAPTER 10

The Senator and His Aide: Compounding Misinformation

For reasons that shall become obvious, I will refer to this former long-standing United States senator as merely "Senator X" and his aide as "Aide Z."

Considered conspicuously liberal, Senator X was a champion of workers and was a driving force behind key labor legislation. He was an aggressive and self-made millionaire but earned a reputation of fighting big business in Washington.

I met him in the early 1990s when he invited many others and me to attend a meeting (not a Senate committee meeting) to discuss the status of the workforce and possible future legislation to protect employee interests.

I had no speaking part and was surprised at what I heard.

His aide introduced the senator and briefly reviewed the senator's record, especially his interest in labor-related issues.

Senator X began by touching on the general need for worker protections. He then made the point that if employers had been more responsible and had treated their employees better, there would have been no need for all the effort he had taken over the years to protect employees through federal legislation.

The Senator used Henry Ford as an example of enlightened and generous employer practices. He used as an example how Henry Ford, during the heart of the Depression, doubled employees' wages.

I was dumbfounded. How could such a famous and brilliant senator get this so wrong?

True, Henry Ford announced that he would pay his factory workers $5 "a day" (not an hour) for eight hours of work. But he did not make this pronouncement during "the heart of the [1930s] Depression." His new pay scale was announced January 5, 1914—twenty years earlier than the senator led his audience to believe. Nor did Henry Ford give his employees this extra money for them to purchase his automobiles, which some have suggested.

The real story behind Ford's generosity is that in the year before he granted this significant increase in pay, he had introduced the concept of an assembly line to his Highland Park, Michigan, factory. He also increased the number of shifts from two to three, growing the number of employees by approximately five thousand people.

These actions greatly increased productivity and allowed him to reduce the price of his automobiles. Ford sales more than doubled, increasing from 89,455 cars in 1912 to 189,088 in 1913. The result: The Ford Motor Co. doubled its net income from $13.5 million in 1912 to $27 million in 1913, according to Allan Nevins, author of *Ford: The Times, the Man, the Company.*

In addition, Nevins wrote, "In July 1914, the company announced that on Aug. 1 its prices would be cut by $60, bringing the runabout to $440, the touring car to $490 and the town car to $690." These reductions were approximately 12 percent, 10 percent, and 8 percent, respectively, for each car.[25]

In regard to the pay increase of $5 per day, it is not certain to whom credit should be given. In their book, *The Fords: An American Epic*, Peter Collier and David Horowitz claim that James Couzens, Mr. Ford's vice president and treasurer, presented a proposal to raise wages from about $2.34 a day to $5.00. They said that Couzens won the Ford founder over by telling him that a $5 daily wage would be the greatest advertising any auto company could have.

However, others who knew the situation confirmed that the idea was Mr. Ford's and his alone. At a minimum, as head of the company, he had to approve such a major increase in pay for workers.

Mr. Ford's thinking also reflected that he wanted the new wage scales to be linked more directly to profits. Customers were getting the benefits of lower costs, while the Ford Company profited like never before. It did not take the genius of Mr. Ford to anticipate that the workers would wonder if and when they were going to have a share in the profits. There were already signs of employee dissatisfaction from other issues.

My first job out of college was in 1962 at the Ford Motor Company. Given my interest and education in labor relations, I was assigned to work at the Ypsilanti plant's labor relations section. At times, I would talk to shop employees who had been with the company thirty years or more, having joined the company during the Depression. Their stories about life at the

---

25 Arlena Sawyers, "$5-a-day Wage Galvanized America and Polished Ford's Image," *Automotive News*, June 26, 1996, http://www.autonews.com/article/20140106/OEM01/140109924/remembering-henry-fords-$5-day-for-line-workers.

Ford Motor Company provided good insight about work at Ford during the Depression.

For instance, one employee told me that to keep his job, he felt obligated to bring a chicken to his supervisor every Friday. Another employee told me that every Friday his supervisor fired someone, without fail. As a result, employees would do whatever they thought they had to do to avoid getting fired. I remember the employee suggesting that, to not be the one terminated on Friday, he would go home for dinner and return to work to volunteer to do additional work, without pay.

Nor was it unusual for the same supervisors to be receptive to allowing an employee terminated under these conditions to return to work, after assurances from the worker that he had learned his lesson, whatever that lesson was. Old service records suggested that, after being terminated, some employees returned to work for the company multiple times.

Nevertheless, the major contributor to high employee turnover was not arbitrary actions by supervisors but the inherent distasteful nature of the work. Mass production was possible only by breaking down the assembly line tasks into simple steps done repeatedly, with ever-increasing speed. The result was that the workers would quickly grow bored of their dumbed-down jobs. Boring jobs on top of poor supervisory practices caused many to quit. The failing retention rate became so serious that in 1913 the annual rate of employee turnover reached a staggering 370 percent.

In 1913, just before the implementation of the $5-a-day wage, to maintain a workforce of about 13,600 workers required hiring 52,000 workers a year. This value was approximately six times greater than even the highest turnover experienced by today's worst U.S. employers.

Ford needed to keep the assembly line rolling regardless of this extremely high turnover rate. The issue of worker turnover, therefore, became critical. The hope was that if the company raised wages high enough, people would be willing to do the work, put up with work-related difficulties, and not quit.

The $5-a-day wage accomplished that goal. The country was in a recession, and the day after the wage increase was announced, 10,000 men reported to Ford's factory seeking employment. The news continued to spread, and within a couple of weeks, as many as 15,000 men showed up at the plant with hopes of obtaining employment.

However, the $5-a-day wage did not come without strings attached. The basic rate would stay at $2.34. The remainder, $2.66, was considered profit sharing to reflect Mr. Ford's linking the bonus to productivity and profitability. In addition, to be eligible for the total of $5.00, employees had to be on the job for six months, be at least twenty-two years old (unless unmarried or supporting a widowed mother or other such relative), and be male.

The most interesting requirement attached to the bonus was Mr. Ford's own values. He wanted to make sure that the additional bonus he paid employees was not squandered. So he set up a "Sociological Department" with investigators to check out employee lifestyles and habits. Ford investigators descended on employees at their homes and asked personal questions about their marital status, nationality, and religion. Investigators wanted to know how much money employees saved, how much they owed and to whom, whether they owned their homes, and what their monthly housing costs were. Gambling, having an unkempt home or yard, and not bathing frequently enough were grounds for forfeiting the bonus. Again, female employees were not included in the initial announcement. Henry Ford later explained that "we expect the young ladies to get married." Women were included in the plan in 1916.[26]

Unfortunately, in those days, when your name was on the building, you could do almost anything.

The Aide

I was concerned for Senator X.

With so many people in a room from other companies, unions, educational institutions, and government, surely others knew what I knew. I thought I had heard the senator suggest that Ford's wage increase was not $5 a day but instead $5 an hour and ensure that the distinction was understood. But the major error was that Ford's surprising, and generous, action was taken in 1914, not "in the heart of the depression" in the 1930s. Also, I felt I should share how Mr. Ford's employee relations record was suspect.

At a break in the proceedings, I approached the senator's aide and quickly highlighted the real facts to him. I expressed my concern about the senator being challenged, possibly subjecting him to embarrassment. The aide thanked me profusely. The meeting resumed, and no clarifications were provided, which was fine with me since my only objective was to have the senator not make the same mistakes again.

The Aide Again

A few weeks later, I was invited to speak at a conference sponsored by the National Association of Temporary and Staffing

---

26 Henry Ford in collaboration with Samuel Crowther, *My Life and Work* (Garden City, NY: Doubleday, Page & Co., 1922), 126-130.

Services (NATS). Senator X's labor agenda was of great interest to NATS and its members. However, this time the senator was not available, so his aide was to represent him.

The aide was to speak first, and I was scheduled to follow him. I could not believe what I heard. The aide started his speech with how wonderful and generous Mr. Ford was, and how he, in the heart of the Depression, increased workers' wages ... etc. When he finished his talk, he left immediately and prior to my advance to the podium.

It was incredible that the aide had repeated the same incorrect statements that his boss had said about Mr. Ford's actions and generosity. However, this time I did not let the aide get away with telling inaccuracies to conference attendees. I told the group that I had previously witnessed what the senator said regarding Henry Ford's generosity and that it was incorrect in several key aspects. In addition, I informed the group that I had previously corrected the senator's misinformation.

Why had the aide repeated the senator's previous incorrect statements after I had informed the aide of the needed corrections? I guess it was because it sounded like a good story, and no one else had ever challenged him. However, nations cannot create legislation based on what is close to a fairy tale. Just like any organizational leader, our lawmakers need to be attentive to the facts. Leaders need to be listeners and learners. Poor facts make poor laws, and laws touch too many lives.

CHAPTER 11

The Competency Equation

This is not a history book. That is not what I am trying to accomplish.

I selected the previous, almost ancient, examples because if individuals did not live through those eras, they inherited them. I chose to revisit these simple but highly visible examples of employer discrimination in the workplace and of poor policies and practices to illustrate how peoples' lives can be negatively influenced not only by intended employer conduct, but also by unintended, uninformed, and poorly directed individuals in positions of influence.

Equally important, I hope readers have caught themselves wondering how management representatives, members of Congress, educators, and others could have permitted such poor practices to exist. Was the inappropriateness of this conduct not clearly seen as unacceptable? The answer is "no," and for the same reasons today's management representatives, and others, are most assuredly missing the current clues of change.

How can we ensure we learn how to avoid such negative impact by improved interpretation of the past, more accurately anticipating the future, and doing the right thing for your employer and yourself?

I have attempted to illustrate how it is not easy to accurately predict the future. Nor is it easy to always do the right thing. What is easy is being ignorant and not trying. Then too, there is Thomas Gray's famous poem that suggests ignorance is bliss—that is unless you are leading.

Requirements, complexities, and expectations within the workforce are increasing. This trend is very unlikely to change, and if anything, will accelerate.

Today more people work in a recognized profession than ever before. Previously, professions were limited to doctors, dentists, lawyers, engineers, scientists, educators, pilots, and other occupations requiring extended education and some type of certification or licensure. Usually, jobs become professions if:

- There is a body of knowledge.
- The body of knowledge can be taught, learned, and tested.
- The profession is recognized globally.
- There is a process for organized research.
- Ethical requirements exist.

In addition, the requirements for most other jobs, even if they are not part of a recognized profession, have increased in terms of education and knowledge required. This shift is quite evident when we examine the significant change in the "blue-collar" versus "white-collar" workforce.

Most nations are shifting from a labor force composed of primarily manual laborers to white-collar and service workers. This trend has been evolving for many years. "The number of workers in professional, technical, and related occupations increased more than fourfold from 1910 until 2000."[27]

That transition is not necessarily more individuals in the workforce; rather it is more competent people in the workforce. There will be no room for the uneducated, untrained, unprepared, and the less-than-committed employee. Those who are not qualified and not ready for more demanding positions are at great risk.

With that in mind, how can we define and advance "competency"?

The Competency Equation Guide[28]

INTELLIGENCE + EDUCATION + EXPERIENCE + ETHICS +/- INTEREST = COMPETENCY

Let us take the components of this equation one by one. First, *intelligence* is what each of us inherits, for example, our capacity to learn, process data, and turn data into information to solve problems. There is not much we can do about the intelligence we possess. Some of us have more. Some of us have less. Relatively little is known about the origin of intelligence. Certainly, genetics plays a significant role, and more recent research suggests that emotional intelligence can also be a factor contributing to one's intelligence.

Emotional intelligence is generally defined as the capacity to be aware of, control, and express one's emotions and to handle interpersonal relationships judiciously and empathetically. It is critical when considering leadership styles and performance. We

---

27 Marlene A. Lee and Mark Mather, "U.S. Labor Force Trends," *Population Bulletin* 63, no. 2 (June 2008): 9, http://www.prb.org/pdf08/63.2uslabor.pdf.

28 The original source for this competency equation was presented by me in the journal article "Mastering the Competencies of HR Management," *Human Resource Management* 38, no. 2 (Summer 1999), 99-102.

have all seen very intelligent people who fail or, at a minimum, underperform, simply because they could not maintain good interpersonal relationships. Especially, in more senior management positions, this inability to perceive, interpret, and respond to the emotions and desires of others can be a serious career inhibitor.

I remember, specifically, a highly placed corporate executive who, after the Burroughs/Sperry merger, turned down our offer to move from New York City to the Philadelphia area as we established a new Unisys corporate headquarters there. We offered him outplacement, and given his senior status, the cost of providing the services was going to be significant.

However, after only a couple of sessions with this individual, the outplacement company found him so aggressive, abrasive, and disruptive that it refused to work further with him. The outplacement firm sent him back to us and returned the payment that we had made for the outplacement services.

I had previously tried to tactfully talk with this individual, a peer, about his interpersonal relationships. Apparently, I had little or no success. His rejection, though, by the outplacement consulting firm gave me the opportunity to talk to him more directly about how he should change, not only to gain alternative employment but also to be a more effective executive.

Notwithstanding my good intentions, the executive was still very defensive and rejected almost every suggestion I made. Again, I warned him that his poor interpersonal relationships with others was definitely hurting his career. To get his attention, I informed him that in all the years I had worked with outplacement firms, never had I seen an outplacement firm accept a client and then subsequently also terminate the person. He finally got the message.

Education complements intelligence. As the second key variable in the competency equation, education may carry the same weight as intelligence. Numerous theories exist about the connections between intelligence and education. It is safe to say, of course, that many people are intelligent, but a part of decision-making requires gathering pertinent facts and information to make sound judgments. After all, you think and solve problems with what you know.

Educational requirements have been significantly raised in our world of work. Sometimes the information age can give us more information than we can use efficiently. In addition, education is no longer thought of as something that is optional or that ends with a degree. It is now a lifelong commitment in which the pursuit of knowledge never ends.

Experience plays an equally important role in competency. Experience, we are taught, is life's greatest teacher. It is not enough, however, to rely on one's own experience and intelligence. Many in management, especially, are guilty of limiting their fact-gathering by drawing on only their personal experience and not adding the experience of others. Why? Sometimes the reason is that they have not worked elsewhere. Sometimes the reason is that they are comfortable with their knowledge and experience. However, if individuals do not take the time to ensure they know the comparative policies and practices of other respected organizations or competitors, they are at great risk. Good managers and leaders must take advantage of as many experiences as possible. Limiting the review of experiences to those in the same organization runs the risk of adding little or nothing new. This is especially true when one organization is challenged to make a change that has already been made by another organization under similar circumstances. In addition to understanding the other organization's best practices, it is important to know what challenges and mistakes the other organization may have experienced as it made its changes. Avoiding someone else's mistakes is a great shortcut. This risk is extremely critical in larger organizations in which professionals and leaders tend to become insulated. Without having the opportunity to gain comparative knowledge about the experiences and best practices of others, the problem-solving abilities of the organization will be disadvantaged.

The power of targeted alternate experience—learning from the experience of others in similar circumstances—cannot be overstated. Also, the ability to tap into this experience has been made exponentially simpler with the advent of the World Wide Web. Today, at essentially no cost, information is instantly available by a few keystrokes.

The competent professional must also use *ethics* to protect the organization from acts that are meant to cause serious harm (such as giving away trade secrets) and his or her own professional reputation from acts meant to benefit the individual (such as embezzlement). Marginally qualified leaders overlook the more subtle forms of unethical behavior—acts that are much more likely, in the long run, to harm both the organization and the individual leader's professional standing. Such behaviors include protecting or enhancing one's position within an organization by not objecting to an issue that the person knows may cause ethical problems. Competitive demands may compound the importance of organizational performance, particularly when the person wants to be viewed as a "team player."

Accusing someone of not being a team player is very frequently confirmation that ethical problems exist with the accuser. Pointing to others' practices to justify what independently might be questioned is like a child suggesting, "Johnny does it, so why can't I?"

Subtle or overt, overlooking unethical activities may provide a false sense of security or hope of organizational success in the short term. However, inconsistencies will be discovered somewhere down the road. When that happens, the individual and the organization will have a tough time establishing credibility again. In short, poor ethics have long-term, damaging effects on competency.

Competency can also be influenced by an inherent *interest* in the job or profession. Interest can have a positive or negative value. Without interest, individuals are less likely to explore their profession and apply themselves effectively, whereas a genuine passion for a trade or profession can have a stunningly beneficial effect on job performance.

For instance, very successful people are often asked to express the key ingredient of their success. Time and time again, they indicate that the greatest contribution to their success is a genuine love of their work. For most of these people, spending hours burning the late-night oil is not the chore it might be for others. It could even be a passion. There is nothing else they would rather be doing! Yes, an occupation is something to be enjoyed, and when it is discovered that it is not, it is time to leave.

CHAPTER 12

Advocacy

Customarily, when we think of the word "advocacy," we think of the political process, usually by a group, which attempts to influence public policy.

The way I wish to define advocacy, within the overall concept of leadership competency, is a leader or individual taking a position on a controversial subject and making things happen in a positive and corrective way.

Unfortunately, management tends to be characteristically hesitant to change policies and practices. Too frequently managers do not see the future, are comfortable with what they know, and have adapted to current policies and practices. Sometimes they simply want to be seen as team players and as avoiding "rocking the boat." They can easily live with policies and practices that a person with a different perspective or experience might assertively challenge.

Hopefully, many reading this book have taken the initiative to speak in favor of a cause, policy, or procedure change, or have witnessed others doing so. However, in an everything-is-okay-here organization, the characteristic of conspicuous objection is often more likely to disadvantage an individual and a career, even when the grievant pleads on behalf of others.

Advocacy can be a key element of performance by advancing ideas that challenge the status quo. However, not everyone is willing to assume the risk of challenging existing management policies and practices, especially when the issue at hand is contrary to the current leaders' experiences and orientation, or entitlement.

The assumption that challenging existing policies and practices is somewhat risky is a good assumption, especially if the individual's overall competency is lacking. For others, especially the true leaders, challenging a practice may confirm not only a person's competency but also the person's ability and willingness to appropriately, and actively, lead and support change that can positively affect the organization and, consequently, many lives.

With change advanced correctly, the advocates who fear losing their heads actually discover they get a "pat on the back." Even if the person suggesting change, or advancing an idea, is rejected, just how that person deals with the rejection is critical. Accepting the rejection with silent disappointment will only serve to fester and sooner or later lead to the person leaving the organization. The loss of competent people with the additional energy and interest to advance change can be deadly to an organization. However, if the person appeals the rejection decision because he or she feels change must occur, even at the risk of irritating senior management, it may be the best thing to do.

For instance, consider when a difficult job must be filled, who is most likely to get the job? Will it be the person who simply takes the orders and does what he or she is told? Or will it be the individual who has a good idea but is knocked down, yet keeps coming back because that person feels what must be done, must be done. Who's more likely to get the new, difficult job—and get it done? Management, shareholders, and employees like leaders who persist and make things happen.

Illustrative Case

The next example is from a long time ago. I resurrect an old situation because only then can the reader examine the case and, with today's knowledge and experience, more quickly recognize the inappropriateness of an issue and the difficulty of initial attempts to introduce change.

The point I have already made is that recognizing change is the most difficult part of leadership. I do not want to write a book that deals merely with theory and offers vague suggestions for future strategies.

My objective is to highlight to everyone how difficult it is to see the future and to challenge past practices. For instance, if in some magical way, a person from 2050 could join us today, how much easier do you think it would be for that individual to challenge our current practices and propose solutions? Delinquency in recognizing the need for change means leaders are making mistakes each day.

The Welder

At New Holland's new manufacturing plant in Nebraska, he was one of the first employees. He was a welder, and a good one. Unlike most of the employees we assigned to the welding department, he was experienced. Others needed substantial training.

In the mid-1960s, our hiring process included a requirement for a physical examination. A local doctor did all of
our physicals and attempted to ensure that all candidates for
employment were physically suitable for the position.

In those days, the physical was also sometimes used
to disqualify people for employment, and not because they
were unsuitable for the job, but because the person had some
preexisting medical condition that could negatively affect the
employer's experience rating for the company's self-insured
health insurance program. In addition, our company specifically identified some conditions that would disqualify an
applicant for employment. One such condition was epilepsy.

One day, an employee came into my office and said to me:
"I thought we did not hire people who have epilepsy." I confirmed that there was a company policy that did preclude the
hiring of people with epilepsy. The employee said this excellent
welder we had on the payroll had epilepsy.

I called the welder into my office and asked him if he had
epilepsy. Tears came to his eyes, and he reluctantly admitted
that he did. I had a problem. First, by policy, he was not
employable by our company. Second, he lied during the
employment process. Third, he was the best welder we had.

I told him to return to work and that the company would
take no action until I had a chance to consider his situation
more fully.

The first thing I did was call our local company doctor.
His response was that our policy about not hiring employees with epilepsy may be inappropriate. The doctor stated if
the candidate had divulged his history of epilepsy, he would
have checked closely to ensure the epilepsy was under control, presumably by medicine. He stated that if the welder's

epilepsy was under control, he would have approved him for employment.

That made sense to me.

At the same time, I thought, "Why had I not thought of that?" A physical examination was a "test," just like a paper and pencil test. Any test is intended to determine whether an applicant could perform satisfactorily as an employee. If we were attempting to validate this test, employees without epilepsy should have succeeded on the job while those who had epilepsy should fail. The employee had not failed—he had excelled.

The only other grounds for disqualifying this employee for employment, and possibly others like him, was to avoid the risks that this condition may contribute to increased absenteeism or health insurance costs. This struck me as unfair—twenty-five years before the Americans with Disabilities Act.

I wrote to our corporate physician, located at our company headquarters in New Holland, Pennsylvania. I outlined the situation and suggested the policy be changed to be consistent with the recommendation of our local doctor in Nebraska. That was, people with epilepsy would not be disqualified automatically. They, like any other applicant's condition, should be eligible for employment if their medical condition was under control.

The doctor rejected my recommendation.

Already having support from my general manager in Nebraska to appeal the corporate doctor's decision, I wrote what became my first position paper. I identified the issue, in this case the policy. I reviewed the history of this policy within our company and identified the arguments on both sides of the issue. The position paper concluded with my recommendation for changing the policy.

This more formalized approach, or appeal, seemed to tie up the issue better. People had to make a conscious decision. They made the decision, and it was in favor of the welder. The policy was changed.

I thanked the welder for being cooperative and confirmed that his employment would be continued and that the policy would be changed. We took no action on the fact that he had failed to divulge his epileptic condition during the employment process. I argued, what option did he have when he knew that this unfair policy existed and would deny him even the opportunity to be considered for employment? It was our inappropriate policy that forced him to lie.

A few years later, my eight-year-old son was diagnosed with epilepsy. Medicine was not effective in controlling his seizures. Some days he experienced multiple seizures. At age sixteen, he had a difficult, eight-hour surgical procedure to remove part of his brain in an attempt to stop or better control the seizures. The surgery was successful. He never had another seizure. More than once, I wondered if what I had done for the welder was our family's reward.

Twenty-five years after my experience with the welder, the Americans with Disabilities Act became law. The law now demanded a new policy for many employers. But not us. We had accurately anticipated the future and had voluntarily established a complying policy many years earlier.

Suggesting appropriate changes, especially in a well-running organization, is also the best way to ensure that your boss does not make a mistake, which is always the optimal contribution to successful performance.

CHAPTER 13

Having Time for One Employee's Issue

The welder's case first appears to be a singular issue affecting but one employee. However, that was not the case. As resolved, the policy could potentially affect many employees. Moreover, future legislative requirements were preempted, and instead a leadership position focused issues on employment of people with disabilities was established. That is a good return on investment anytime.

Other times, it may appear difficult to achieve a return on investment when dealing with only one individual and his or her situation. My experience suggests, however, that there is a different type of return on investment. It is touching someone's life, often when the person does not even seek assistance. Assistance provided to someone at work, or in general, can pay big dividends. Frequently those people, or their situations, later affect the leader more than the leader helped them.

Ollie's Holiday Pay

Within two weeks of joining the New Holland division of Sperry Corporation, everyone was on holiday—Labor Day.

A few days after we returned to work, I noticed there was a "buzz" going around the plant. Based on my experience, a buzz is when something has happened and employees are talking about it in a somewhat guarded way, because no one wants to ask or challenge management directly. Others characterize this old, loose, informal communications process as "the grapevine." Rather than allowing an issue to fester, especially in the shop, I was determined to identify the problem.

The problem was that an employee, Ollie, was told he would not receive holiday pay for the Labor Day holiday because he had not worked the day after Labor Day. I was reminded there was a strict rule for employees to qualify for holiday pay: They had to work the day before and the day after the holiday. This rule, presumably, was to ensure that employees would not arbitrarily extend their holiday, leaving the company's production process compromised.

When I asked why Ollie was not at work the day after Labor Day, I learned the reason was that he was attending his mother's funeral.

I could not believe that Ollie was going to be penalized for this absence. It was not fair, was inconsistent with the practices of other employers, and made no sense. How, for instance, could the company pay Ollie for the funeral leave, but at the same time, use the excused funeral absence as a reason to disqualify the employee for his holiday pay?

I discussed the situation with Ollie's supervisor, who was sympathetic but warned me this policy was strictly administered, and no exceptions were permitted. The supervisor suggested that I talk to payroll.

I talked to payroll, which said same thing: no exceptions. I told payroll staff members that no other company I knew administered a holiday pay policy like that. Their recommendation was to go up the line and talk to the general manager of the plant, my boss, Frank Powl. That I did.

Again, I was new to the company, and Frank had only been my boss for two weeks. We hardly knew each other. I made my case to him about Ollie's situation. He admitted that some of my logic made sense, but then defaulted to the excuse one uses when all of his or her logic fails. That is, "Mike, when you are here longer, you will understand." Rather than being discouraged, I immediately felt such a philosophy was sufficient justification to examine the appropriateness of any policy that used that reasoning as the defense. Then, for good measure, he added, "And anyway, Bob would never approve it."

I did not have to ask who Bob was because he was the first New Holland management person that I had met. He was the VP for manufacturing, Frank's boss, and the individual to whom my former professor at the University of Michigan had recommended me.

Bob Ressler invited me to come to this small town of New Holland, in the heart of the Pennsylvania Dutch area, to be interviewed by him. He had assigned Frank the task of picking me up at the Philadelphia airport and taking me to New Holland for a Saturday morning interview.

Every mile of the highway between the Philadelphia airport and New Holland, Frank thoroughly educated me about Mr. Ressler. He emphasized how Bob was a self-made man, starting off originally as an hourly paid toolmaker for what was then Armstrong Cork Company. George Delp, the key New Holland founder, witnessed Ressler umpiring a baseball game. Mr. Delp was impressed with how Ressler had handled a disputed call and hired him as one of the first New Holland employees. Ressler grew with the company.

Bob had a reputation of being blunt, but honest and highly credible. Apparently, more than once, a disgruntled plant worker went to Ressler's home on a Sunday afternoon asking to talk to him about some type of problem at the plant. He always had time for the worker. The affectionate name given to him by the workers was "Sunny Old Bob." Figure out those initials.

I knew that it would be Sunny Old Bob who would determine if I got the job or not. After I walked into his office, with Frank, I had very little hope.

Mr. Ressler did not get up from his desk. He quickly glanced at me, and I recognized an obvious disappointment. I did not know what I had done or what could possibly have gone wrong since I had not even said one word yet and had not even shaken his welcoming hand.

Then he grilled me. He asked me all kinds of questions, including what was my religion, what was my wife's religion, what were my politics, what were my wife's politics, and other questions that were personal and not appropriate even then.

This went on for more than an hour. Finally, he paused, and I discovered what he did not like about me. He said: "When you walked in here, you were too short."

So Bob could be difficult and arbitrary. Is this what it takes to be the type of person who would not give Ollie his holiday pay because he was at his mother's funeral?

Ollie's Holiday Pay—A Second Chance!

Shortly after Frank, my boss, and I discussed Ollie's situation, Frank told me that Bob wanted to introduce me to some of his peers, the other vice presidents. Frank and I went down to Bob's office at the New Holland headquarters. Once there, Bob separately invited the various officers of the company into his office and introduced me to each one.

Then he invited in J. Paul Lyet, the chief financial officer of our division, who would later become the chairman of Sperry Corporation. He was one of the most respected management representatives in our division. Lyet walked into Bob's office rather aggressively, shook my hand, and then immediately—and I mean immediately—asked, "If you could change one of our employee policies, what would it be?"

All I could think of was the stupid policy that would not permit Ollie to be paid his holiday pay.

I was very surprised by the question. With my boss and Ressler there, I tried to finesse the situation by reminding him I was new to the company. I told him I looked forward to "reviewing the employee-related policies and making recommendations at a later date."

Lyet acknowledged that I had been there only several weeks but asked again if I had even an early feeling or opinion about New Holland's people approach. I looked at Bob who, with squinted eyes, was also looking directly at me, wondering what I might say. I looked at Frank, my boss, who I suspect was even more worried about what I might say and if Bob would approve.

But then I thought the HR God had brought Lyet and his question into this meeting for a purpose.

I started to make my case about Ollie and how New Holland's holiday pay policy was inappropriate and should be changed. In rapid fire, I shared all of my arguments:

- A New Holland employee attending a qualifying family member's funeral is covered by a separate, rather flexible and generous, funeral leave policy, which provides for a reasonable, not specified, amount of excused paid absence to arrange and attend the funeral.

- I told him how Ollie had been denied his Labor Day holiday pay because he was on funeral leave the next day to attend his mother's funeral—an excused, paid absence.

- I emphasized that I knew of no other company that would do this.

- I added that if New Holland had a union, there would be no way the company could defend a union challenge on this practice. I added, "If you want a union, just keep up this type of practice."

- I added that Ollie was going to work at the company for many more years. I asked if it was worth applying this aggressive interpretation of the policy only to have each anniversary of his mother's death remind him of how the company treated him.

- I suggested there was a good chance this type of policy could have a significant negative impact on other employees' opinions about the company, possibly affecting their dedication to quality and productivity.

- I concluded that it was also the company practice for a management representative to attend the funeral and to offer his or her condolences on behalf of the company. But was that not contradictory and awkward under these circumstances?

As I took a breath, Mr. Lyet had apparently heard enough. He turned to look at Sunny Old Bob and asked, "Bob, do we do that?"

Bob's response was immediate and with gusto: "Not anymore!"

I literally walked out of Bob's office with Ollie's holiday pay. However, much more than that occurred on our ride home. Frank was driving and quiet. I feared he might be upset by the way I handled myself. In contrast, illustrating the type of gentleman he was, he said to me, "Mike, I forgot why we brought you here. I'm not saying I'm always going to agree with you, but I promise you I will listen better."

I knew what he meant. He knew that I had an education in my chosen profession. He knew I also had good work experiences that gave me an appreciation of comparative practices. He and I both learned that day how to offer a different perspective and possibly get a policy changed—even if it was for only eight hours of holiday pay for one employee.

Possibly, he also recognized that he may have let down his boss, Bob. More specifically, Frank failed to accurately anticipate Sunny Old Bob's response. He assumed Bob "would never" change the policy when, in fact, it took Bob but a millisecond to change the policy once he knew the circumstances and the attendant facts.

For me, it was the first time that I found it necessary to assertively challenge a company policy. It was addictive, and Frank, and others, did listen more carefully.

The greatest impact, however, was unanticipated.

That buzz that was ricocheting around our plant changed. Now the message was this: "That new, short guy from personnel went down to see Sunny Old Bob and came back with Ollie's holiday pay."

I could not have gained the workers' and management's confidence more effectively.

Lester

How much time does a leader have for the employee who is not performing satisfactorily, possibly needs mentoring, or may have a disability or some other personal issue?

Even more difficult is the demand or opportunity put on a leader to provide personal assistance when someone is not an employee.

I learned that lesson early, also.

I did not know who he was, but I saw his head abruptly appear in the doorway of my office. I was busy, but this person was obviously upset, and his face communicated a sense of urgency. My secretary stopped him from continuing into my office and asked him to have a seat.

With an increasing level of curiosity, I finished my current task and invited him into my office. He was an applicant for employment, and I was still the personnel manager for New Holland's plant in Lancaster, Pennsylvania, again, a Civil War-era facility that barely met the requirements for manufacturing anything.

Before he sat down, he started talking a hundred miles an hour. To this day, I can remember the barrage: "I don't want to fill out an application (for employment) if you are not going to consider me. I have been in prison for stealing a car, which also got me dishonorably discharged from the Navy. When I got out of prison, the owner of [name of company withheld] hired me. He is really religious, and he has hired others like me, but I just do not like it there. He keeps pushing his religion on me."

I told him to calm down and promised to take the necessary time to consider him for employment. I was willing to do that partly because of the bizarre way he had presented himself, and we desperately needed employees.

We had only recently announced that we were going to close this particular plant and move the operations to a new facility in Grand Island, Nebraska. The problem was that we had to continue production until the new manufacturing facility in

Nebraska was ready. We had already established a retention program providing special benefits to those employees who stayed with us until the plant was closed.

Of course, recruiting new employees is difficult when the first thing you must tell them is that the plant is closing. This already resulted in the company, to some extent, lowering its standards for employment. However, not so low to welcome someone who had served time in prison and got kicked out of the Navy.

But I listened.

His story was long. Disadvantaged as a child, he joined the Navy. While on leave one weekend, he stole a car and was caught, convicted, and sent to prison. That was the end of his Navy career.

Lester then told me that he had changed while in prison. He had a prior tendency to be defensive and combative, but he claimed that he started to realize that if he did not change his conduct, he would be at risk, first by continued difficulties with other convicts and also by disadvantaging his chances of parole. The last thing I needed was to take a lot of time to check and otherwise consider this applicant. However, I did. I called the prison, and the prison official confirmed that Lester, when he arrived in prison, was difficult to handle. He was reprimanded and punished more than once. The prison authorities were very helpful and confirmed everything Lester had said, including that Lester's behavior had improved over time.

The next thing I did was talk to the machine shop management that would provide his supervision if we hired him. Because Lester had told me one of the problems he had on his prior job was people knowing he was an "ex-con" and making life at work difficult, I did not inform his prospective supervisors that he had been imprisoned, nor did I reference what happened in the Navy. I merely told the supervisors that Lester had had some problems but that I had carefully checked him out. As desperate as we were for people, I recommended we give him a chance. He was interviewed by the supervisors, who said they would take him.

He was scheduled to work on the night shift, and, rather than having him report directly to his new supervision, I asked him to see me first. He knew that he was being given a break because he had been rejected by so many other companies. I reminded him about the plans to close the plant in about nine months. I suggested if he did a good job with us, at a minimum, he would gain a favorable job reference from a good company.

We also had an incentive program whereby production employees could increase their compensation if they produced in excess of the established production standard. As in most companies with production incentive programs, employees are careful not to abuse it. In other words, no one materially exceeded the production required for fear that would only invite an increase in the standard itself. I told Lester to ignore this presumption because we were closing the plant anyway. I told him to work as hard as he could, producing as much as he could, and he would be able to substantially increase his compensation.

Then I held my breath.

After that I did not see him that often because he was on the night shift. Then one day he came to my office and showed me his paycheck. He said it was the largest paycheck he had ever received. He told me he was on his way to a check cashing service down the street. Knowing that the check cashing service would charge him a modest fee to cash what was obviously a valid payroll check from a respected local employer, I asked why he did not just go to the bank nearby.

He acted as if it had never occurred to him and admitted that he had at no previous time had a bank account. I escorted him into the bank, and he was able to open an account. Now he also had a checking account, for the first time ever.

One night someone broke into the Coca-Cola machine that was in the factory. The next day, Lester came to work early. He stuck his head around my office door as he had done when we first met, and he said only five words, "I did not do it!" He turned and left, not waiting for a reply.

Then his wife was hospitalized for a brief time. By now, he was on the company health insurance plan. It was the first time he ever had health insurance. He volunteered to me how nice it was to walk into the hospital as a New Holland employee, with health insurance, and be welcomed—a major change from what he experienced in the past. His self-esteem was improving during that time.

On occasion, he would go fishing with his brother, and I would be the beneficiary of one or two fish.

Unfortunately, the scheduled closing of our manufacturing facility in Lancaster was finally approaching. We had already committed to transfer as many employees as we could from our Lancaster plant that we were closing to the major manufacturing plant in New Holland, Pennsylvania, about ten miles away.

Lester never expressed an interest to transfer to the New Holland plant primarily, I believe, because he knew I had given him a chance few others would provide him, considering his background and problems. He did not want to get me in trouble, I suspected.

But then it happened. I received a telephone call from the home office in New Holland, Pennsylvania, telling me to send

Lester's employment file to headquarters. There was no explanation associated with the order to send this file. I anxiously
awaited, and I must admit was somewhat concerned what I had
done would be discovered.

Finally, I got the word. I was told Lester's brother cut the
grass and did other jobs for one of the companies' vice presidents. Apparently, the brother told the vice president how I had
given Lester a break and how well he was doing with his new
employment opportunity with New Holland. At the same time,
the brother confirmed that Lester had not applied for transfer
to the other plant for fear the headquarters management would
react differently.

Instead of me getting into trouble, the headquarters management gave me considerable credit for helping Lester. Instead of
sanctions, I was given praise. Lester did successfully transfer to the
larger New Holland plant after we closed the Lancaster facility.

After moving to Grand Island, Nebraska, and our new
manufacturing plant, I received a call from Lester. He wanted
to come to Nebraska and work for New Holland there. By
this time, he had the job at the New Holland plant and, to my
knowledge, was doing satisfactorily.

Given the substantial distance and costs involved in relocat-
ing from Pennsylvania to Nebraska, the company had a policy
of not permitting existing Pennsylvania employees to transfer
to any other plant, including Grand Island, where we needed
new employees desperately. Why did the policy exist? The company simply did not wish to encourage employees to transfer
to another plant, even at their own cost, for fear such a distant
transfer would not work out for the employee.

I told Lester that transferring to Nebraska was not being
permitted except for management and other professional per-

sonnel. I did not challenge the policy. After all, such transfer requests were rare anyway. He accepted my rejection. I did not appeal or suggest changing the policy.

Regrettably, however, the story does not end there.

Lester hurt his back at work and was off on workers' compensation leave. To supplement his workers' compensation payments, he took a part-time job as a driver for a Lancaster taxi company. One night he accidentally struck a child who later died of the injuries incurred.

Lester lost his job.

I never heard from him again, and although I had tried to locate him, I was unsuccessful.

Yes, it was only one employee, but the policy not to permit transfers, for any reason, bothered me more. If I had worked harder to allow Lester to transfer, his life may have been better.

That was more than fifty years ago, and I have regretted ever since that I did not do more to help Lester come to Nebraska.

Yes, I had touched his life in a good way but then did not do enough. I experienced the joy of helping someone else, but also the disappointment of what I had not done.

Chet Seig

About a year later, enough time to reflect on what had happened to Lester, I experienced a similar situation.

My associate came into my office and told me that there was a gentleman in the waiting room who wanted to see me, and he said he knew me. When I asked who, she said it was Chet Seig.

Chet Seig, I thought, "He is here?"

Chet had worked for us on the 717 forage harvester assembly line in Lancaster and never did much to bring attention to himself, except be a quiet, good employee.

I quickly brought him into my office, anxious to welcome him. We started to talk. He had transferred to the New Holland plant, so he was able to continue with the company after we closed the Lancaster plant. I asked him if he was on vacation, and he told me he had taken time off of work to come to Nebraska to see me. Chet said he wanted to move to Nebraska and work for New Holland.

I went through the discouragement argument—that Nebraska was a long way from Pennsylvania; we were not encouraging hourly employees to transfer. Even if we allowed employees to come to Nebraska to work for us, they would have to quit their current position with the company and start over at our new facility. Given the fact that Chet already had about fifteen years of service with the company, this was not a small issue.

He listened. Then he started to cry.

I was dumbfounded. Sitting in front of me was a worker I knew well. A tough-looking, short, potbellied ordinary worker who, when he worked, constantly had a very short, unlit cigar hanging out the side of his mouth. I did not need to ask why he was crying. He quickly volunteered, "Mike, all I know is the 717."

No long discussions were required. And I recognized immediately how major change had threatened him.

At the same time, again, it struck me how stupid our policy was. First, I recalled how I had discouraged Lester. Now, here was a long-term employee who wanted to continue to work for the company in a job he knew, appreciated, liked, and performed exceptionally in. Furthermore, he would pay his own way to relocate the 1,200-plus miles to maintain his employment relationship.

This conversation occurred before the Japanese taught us that the worker knows the job best. Japan was going to show us how much the "ordinary" employee could help quality and production efforts. The contributions of worker "quality circles" were already legendary and being copied around the world.

It did occur to me that Chet might be able to help us greatly.

The people on the new Nebraska 717 forage harvester assembly line were having great difficulties getting their production levels up to the required eight or nine machines a day. We had to get these machines to the dealers, who had to deliver them to the farmer customer. Crops do not wait on production delays!

The 717 assembly line was much different from the very familiar moving assembly line on which the auto companies make dozens of automobiles each hour, hundreds in a day. In such an operation, an employee may install only one or two items as the car on the assembly line constantly moves forward.

With the much lower farm equipment volume, there was no moving assembly line. Each worker had a workstation at which the employee assembled numerous parts. An employee could easily spend forty or more minutes on each machine at his station. When done, a hoist moved the machine to the next station. There were only five or six stations.

When we told our new Nebraska employees that in Pennsylvania, workers had consistently manufactured as many as twelve units a day, they simply did not believe us. It verged on management being accused of being unreasonable and having unfair expectations.

I told Chet to wait a minute while I left the room. I went directly to see the general manager, my boss, Frank Powl. I made my case. Frank was hesitant. I pleaded and argued, what did we have to lose? We were not meeting our production requirements, and a growing employee relations problem was developing. I suggested to Frank that Chet's former supervisor, who was still the supervisor for the 717 line now in Nebraska, would certainly welcome Chet. Yes, I argued Chet could help us. Frank reluctantly agreed.

I informed Chet that as soon as he could make the trip to Grand Island, we would put him on the payroll. He knew he was "starting over" but did not complain. He was back in a couple of weeks, and his welcoming supervisor immediately put him at the last station of the 717 assembly line.

The first thing that the other employees noticed was Chet's assortment of tools. In those days, employees were expected to provide their own tools (a reflection of craftsman status; it also did wonders keeping employees from losing or misplacing tools).[29] Chet had an assortment of tools that he used effectively. Little things we did not realize started to become obvious, such as his discipline of always knowing where a particular tool was, rather than laying a tool down and then searching for it when needed again.

Right away, Chet was more efficient than the Nebraska employees. Soon he was going back up the assembly line help-ing others and providing productive hints on how to be more effective with the assembly requirements. Production soon returned to the twelve assembled harvesters per day Chet had experienced previously and, from a compensation perspective, enjoyed. The employees on the assembly line, including Chet, earned bonuses.

Soon, additional employees were asking if this short, potbel-lied guy with the cigar hanging out of his mouth could come to their product's assembly line and give them some helpful hints

---

29 The company had a list of suggested basic tools. If the employee needed tools, he or she could acquire the tools from the company through payroll deduction.

also. Chet did more to improve production performance than almost anyone else, including the plant's general manager.

Chet married a woman who also worked for New Holland. He continued to work for New Holland until his retirement and relocation to Republican City, Nebraska, to a new home on Harlan Lake.

I saw him recently as New Holland was planning the 50th anniversary of the establishment of the plant in Grand Island. I reminded everyone of their important contributions. For Chet, I told him our efforts to allow him to come to Nebraska and work for us was one of the best things we ever did. He just smiled.

Fritz

Fritz was a toolmaker—one of the best.

He emigrated from Germany after World War II and had worked for New Holland many years before I got there. At the time, he was considered a nonexempt employee, paid by the hour.

We desperately needed him to go to Nebraska when we closed the plant in Lancaster, where he worked. We reevaluated his job and promoted him to a salaried, exempt professional position. That would also allow him to be a company-supported candidate for transfer to Nebraska.

I worried, however, he would not wish to transfer all the way to Nebraska. When I asked him that question, his response surprised me. He said, "Mike, when you stand in front of your home in Germany and say good-bye to everyone to go to America, going to Nebraska is nothing!"

As anticipated, Fritz made a major contribution in Nebraska. Unfortunately, he subsequently developed heart trouble. He was off on disability and urgently needed open-heart surgery.

He had already been taken from Grand Island to Omaha for specialized medical attention and the surgery. His surgery was scheduled, but the weekend prior to the planned surgery a major accident occurred, and the blood needed for Fritz's surgery was depleted, leaving not enough blood for Fritz's procedure.

His family was very concerned about the delay. All of us at the company who had come to love him, were concerned also. What could we do as a company?

I called the local Red Cross in Grand Island. There was nothing it could do.

Having had considerable experience coordinating blood drives at my prior employer, the Ford Motor Company, I knew we surely had enough people on our payroll to provide the necessary thirty pints of blood needed for the surgery. How could we get it?

Again, our local company doctor, Dr. Koefoot, came to my rescue. After hearing the story, he agreed to come to the plant and draw blood samples from employee volunteers to see whose blood matched Fritz's blood. Those identified as having the correct blood match were ready to travel the 150 miles to Omaha, on a company-sponsored bus, to donate the blood needed.

Although we had made no attempt to communicate this effort outside the company, when we arrived in Omaha, the TV cameras were rolling. Apparently, the hospital recognized our effort as very special. Possibly, it could serve as an example for other company-sponsored efforts.

Fritz had his surgery the next day and came through it wonderfully. He returned to work a few weeks later.

Unfortunately, a few years after his surgery, and after my return to Pennsylvania to work at the New Holland headquarters, Fritz passed away.

Subsequently, Fritz's wife, who had been an accountant in Germany, was hired to work at the Grand Island plant. She, too, was a great worker.

Then there was their son. He worked for New Holland as a summer engineering college intern in Pennsylvania. Soon the son would be graduating, and for personal reasons, Fritz's wife requested a transfer back to Pennsylvania. There was a job for her at the home office, but the receiving management in the manufacturing division insisted that if Fritz's wife transferred back to Pennsylvania she would need to start over as a new employee.

By this time I had been promoted to the home office headquarters. It was time to change this stupid policy I had seen before with the Lester and Chet Seig cases.

I talked to the VP of manufacturing and highlighted that this policy was, in addition to being unfair, not competitive with other companies' practices. He refused to change this old, outdated policy, which had historically been applied only in the manufacturing division. He did so, I thought, more to protect his "turf" from staff influence than from any possible merit related to the policy.

It was time for another position paper. I distributed the position paper prior to our regular weekly meeting of the North American operating division heads, in other words, purchasing, finance, HR, manufacturing, engineering, information systems, etc.

Given the highly visible and somewhat controversial nature of the position paper, the meeting started with this subject. Initially, the manufacturing division head suggested this issue was no big deal, and he would do whatever the group decided. Then he started his defense by reminding everyone he was the

VP of manufacturing in North America and, with skill and body language, displayed his strong objection to any change.

The debate went back and forth for a long and unnecessary period of time.

The North American president, Mac McCarty, ended the debate. He suggested we had talked about this issue enough. No vote required. He announced the policy would be changed, and the transferring employee's prior service with New Holland would be recognized. This change also applied to Chet Seig, whose situation would be retroactively adjusted.

I do not remember ever having to write a position paper again.

Will You Help My Boyfriend?

A young woman in our purchasing department stopped by my office to ask me if I could assist her and her boyfriend. She informed me that her boyfriend was totally blind. A high school graduate, the only employment he could find was feeding the hogs for his uncle, for which he was paid $25 a week.

They wanted to get married, but under the current circumstances that was not possible. Having him employed would help greatly.

She anticipated that our company may not have an appropriate employment opportunity for him. She merely asked that I talk to him and see if I could assist in any way in terms of advice and counsel.

After work one night, she went home and brought him back to my office. He was a fine young man. I suggested that hopefully he could look for employment at a mass-production company whose jobs would involve highly repetitive tasks. Possibly, in an unchanging environment he could be oriented and trained enough to perform a regular job.

Knowing many of the other companies in the area, I had a specific company in mind. I told him to give me a little time. I called the owner of the company, and he agreed, as I had done, to interview this young man. The interview was successful, and the owner offered him a job. He was to start in a couple of weeks.

Very much wondering how things went, I did not want to ask the woman who worked for us what happened. I did, however, call my friend at the company that was going to hire him, and discovered, to my dismay, that the young man did not show up when he was scheduled to start work.

I was really miffed. I had gone to all this trouble, and he did not show up. Why he did not show up was unknown. I did not want to ask.

Then the young man's girlfriend, our employee, visited me. She thanked me for what I had done but informed me that she was quitting. Her boyfriend had been so encouraged by being offered a job that he applied for a special, government-sponsored program for people with disabilities. He was granted a college scholarship. They were getting married and moving to Colorado so that he could go to college.

Never before had I experienced such joy when someone quit.

CHAPTER 14

Globally Touching People's Lives: It Will Not Work in My Country

Brazil is a long distance from the United States. However, you are generally traveling directly south versus east for Europe or west for the Pacific. The benefit is remaining more or less in your own time zone if you are traveling from the United States. This is a welcome relief from the 115 times I crossed the many time zones to Europe. Counting only the hours to go over and then return, I have calculated that I have spent the equivalent of one work year, more than 2,000 hours, sitting on airplanes just going to Europe and back. This is not counting going to Canada, Mexico, South American, Asian, African, and Middle Eastern countries. Nor does this include time going to the airport, sitting at the airport, staying in a hotel, or working in the foreign country. Is it fun? No. Is it challenging? Yes, sometimes. Is it difficult to perform well in a global setting? Not necessarily.

I clearly remember, however, that prior to my first trip to Europe, I was, though not terrified, traveling without the level of confidence that I customarily maintained in the United States.

I went with my boss, who was introducing me to our global operations. My role was not to talk that much, which was easy to do. However, a curious French, almost-English-speaking general manager interrupted a discussion we were having on an issue, and he specifically asked me for my opinion. I gave him my opinion. That opinion was very similar, if not identical, to what I would have said in the United States. He accepted and praised my response.

I was to later discover winning global acceptance of a recommendation, policy, or practice was not always that easy.

Providing leadership guidance and control in multiple nations can sometimes be a challenge. The challenge of following global best practices is not so overwhelming if the leader is a good leader in his or her home country. All that is needed is a reasonable understanding of comparative practices in the various countries for which the person must attempt to provide leadership. Then the goal is to follow the best practices and to avoid what has not worked satisfactorily in other similar situations and countries. The best contribution a leader can make is the most important characteristic of good management—anticipating the future, because not all nations are on the same timeline.

I learned this lesson when, in the 1970s, I was given HR responsibilities in Europe, South America, Australia, and Japan, in addition to North America. One of my first challenges occurred in Curitiba, Brazil. I was met at the airport by the new Brazilian HR director for our recently completed manufacturing operation in that city. Our company's worldwide vice president of manufacturing had sent me to Brazil to make sure that our new HR professional got off on the right foot and to evaluate his capabilities.

At the time, Brazil was under a military dictatorship with an incredibly high inflation rate and other problems. Nevertheless, it was a large developing country with major growth opportunities and a crucial commitment to eventual democracy.

The Brazilian HR director was an experienced HR professional who had previously worked in the construction industry. He spoke no English, which I did not consider was a major issue. I had learned years previously that an effective meeting depends on who is in the meeting, and specifically their experience and capabilities. Having the capacity to speak English may be a convenient benefit and in some cases even a requirement. However, there is no assurance that a room full of English-speaking managers will yield the best decisions. The best decisions come from those who have the most to contribute. In a global environment, failing to ensure the participation and advance the opinions of those who do not speak English is everyone's loss.

The HR director and a translator met me at the Curitiba airport baggage claim area.

Before even saying "hello" or shaking hands, the Brazilian HR director aggressively said something. Of course, I did not know what he had said.

The translator could not hide her reaction. This signaled to me that she was surprised by the question or statement, and hesitant to translate what he had said. The local HR director, however, insisted. Thus, she repeated the statement in English: "United States personnel practices will not work in Brazil."

Yes, those were the absolute first words out of his month.

My initial thought was, "This is going to be a long week."

We took things slowly. Since we intended to hire more than one thousand employees, the employment process was very important. When I asked questions about the planned employment policies and procedures, he had excuses for why practices in other countries would not work or were not necessary in Brazil.

I soon grew concerned because our top management was particularly anxious to create the type of culture that had worked well for us in the United States—a culture characterized by an interest in each and every employee and a policy to avoid unionized status, whenever possible.

Fortunately, New Holland had been purchased and reorganized by a small group of individuals in 1940, and not previously. The National Labor Relations Act, which gave workers the right to join a union and provided certain protections against employers' unfair labor practices, had already been law for five years before the group acquired the company. By then, the poor employee relations practices and abuses of some employers were well defined by this corrective legislation. Poor employee relations practices did not need to be continued by an enlightened employer—especially one trying to start a new company.

The founders of the reorganized New Holland Machine Company, as it was called then, were indeed men with high moral and ethical standards. However, they were not your typical, highly educated executives with substantial and varied experience.

One was a former barber, one was a Mennonite bishop, and the first president, George Delp, an administrator at a local manufacturing company, earning $40 a week. By nature, they were conservative, religious people who thought getting a brand new company off the ground and winning employee support could be more successfully accomplished without a union. The New Holland management and many other smart leaders of newly created companies took positive actions to avoid those earlier poor practices. They directed emphasis at creating a working environment of shared interests between owners and workers. One way to look at it is that, with substantial challenges to overcome as they started their new company, the last thing the New Holland leaders needed was the requirement to negotiate with a union and compromise their opportunity to act quickly, lead, and work cooperatively with employees.

Gaining employees' trust was not initially easy because resources were scarce. For instance, workers' pay was far from generous. What the leaders did have was good intentions and the willingness to communicate regularly with employees. They established regular meetings to keep employees informed of the company's progress.

Coming from Ford, I was dumbfounded that the company would take employees off the job and that the plant manager and other officials would conduct the employee meeting. The objective was to ensure that, when employees went home to the dinner table, the worker would not need to complain about another abusive day at work. Instead, the hope was the employee would share with the family the company's progress, problems, objectives, and opportunities.

Simply stated, the leaders did not want, as was the case with many other companies at the time, the company to be the enemy.

The impact of the company's practices was not to be underestimated. For instance, the value of key management knowing each employee's name was considered very important. With my prior employer being the Ford Motor Company, I at first thought this was an unreasonable request. But then the person I was hired to replace took me on a tour through the plant and office and introduced me, by name, to every one of the 500 employees at our location. I got the message. I learned all the names.

Another visible difference in employee relations practices was experienced at Christmas, only a few months after I was hired. I learned that one of my tasks was to participate in the Christmas bonus line.

Rooted in the very early days of the company, to show appreciation for the employees' efforts when the company was struggling with start-up problems, the founders decided to provide a Christmas bonus. The bonus was small but highly symbolic.

The top management would have the employees come to the conference room, led by their supervisor. The supervisor was the first to extend the company's appreciation for the employee's effort during the year. Each employee would then continue to the next management representative, the HR person, and the plant manager and finally (at Headquarters) shake the president's hand.

The first year the bonus was handed out in silver dollars, after J. Henry Fisher, the Mennonite bishop, suggested this be done so when the employees went to spend the bonus, the stores would know that the customer worked for New Holland.[30]

I stood in that line for many years, and even after George Delp, the chair and founder, retired, he would return to be in the bonus line. Burley, strong workers with iron handshakes remembered George and would sometimes have tears in their eyes. If older workers said they were going to retire, George would, with joking but sincere appreciation, inform them they

---

30 When the silver dollars ran out for the thousands of employees working for New Holland, the company bonus was handed out with one silver dollar, followed by a check for the remainder of the bonus.

could not do so because the company simply needed them too much.

Many might find such a personal effort by management not just very visible and symbolic but contrived. Contrived it was not. I will always remember spending Christmas with an aching hand and arm after shaking the hand of greater than 2,000 employees at headquarters. Yes it was a tradition that had become culture. The company was different than others, and the employees knew it. This fact was critical, given the fact that in the agricultural industry, all the major producers of farm machinery, except New Holland, were unionized.

With that background and orientation, I made the discussion of employee relations, Brazil's labor laws, and organized labor the last subject with the Brazilian HR director.

On the previous Brazilian HR subjects, I had frequently acquiesced and did not aggressively challenge the gentleman's explanation as to why Brazilian human resource management practices differed substantially from those in the United States and other countries. When I started the topic about the unions in Brazil, I had already known that technically, the unions were recognized by the government, but this recognition was modeled after the labor codes of the Italian dictator, Mussolini, of many years earlier.

Under the Brazilian military dictatorship system, relatively weak unions failing to achieve desired employer concessions would present their demands to the government. The employers then presented to the government their opposition to the union demands. The government would then facilitate a process to provide an eventual resolution of the differences, frequently by government mandate, if necessary. In that way, strikes were avoided, and inflation was somewhat controlled.

As the new HR director reviewed Brazil's labor laws and practices with me, he suggested the unions were relatively weak. He did, however, mention one union leader in the steelmaking industry. He implied that this man was a troublemaker who was very aggressive and was attempting to attract many worker followers. His actions resulted in the government jailing him for a period of time. That labor leader went by one name, Lula.

Recognizing that Brazil was on the path to a full-fledged democracy, I anticipated that the various unions would become stronger and their rights to organize workers more fully protected. I anticipated if a history of poor employer-employee relations practices existed, Brazil could experience some of the problems that existed in other countries when unions gained more power and influence.

He totally disagreed, suggesting the unions were no risk whatsoever, either in the short or long term.

I pursued this line of questioning, and, from a hypothetical standpoint, I pushed back and asked, "What would happen if a strong union simply did not agree with management and the government and insisted on striking to obtain its demands?"

Continuing his impatient disappointment, he put two fingers in front of his face vertically and then crossed those two fingers by two fingers from his other hand. I had no idea what he was doing.

The translator spoke up. She said, "He means the government will simply put the labor leaders in jail."

That was the end of him. We could not depend on such harsh treatment and indifferent management to advance and protect our intended employee relations policies and practices.

While I was in Brazil, I was introduced to a young man who was about twenty-one and was studying to be a lawyer while working part time for us. He had been an exchange student and had lived in Shelby, North Carolina, for a year as a senior in high school. His name was Haroldo Pinto.

I told the general manager to give me this young man for a few weeks, and I would make him an HR person. We did just that.

Haroldo returned to Brazil and started to implement what we considered were the excellent employee relations practices the company used in the United States and other countries. Soon he reported that other local companies were contacting him to see exactly how and why these new initiatives were being implemented. Next, a local personnel association was created for the networking and exchange of information.

Haroldo performed very well. Subsequently, he was made the director of marketing and sales for Brazil. A couple of years after that, he was promoted to New Holland's United States corporate offices with responsibility for Latin America and then on to the high-priority position of a product manager.

He was so good that a competitor, J.I. Case, recruited him. He also distinguished himself at that company. Then, he went on to Textron before becoming the CEO of a large manufacturing company.

Today, more than forty years later, he is one of my closest friends.

Yes, we proved that improved human resource practices could work in Brazil.

And what happened to Lula, the dreaded labor leader? Luiz Inácio Lula da Silva became the president of Brazil in January 2003 and served eight years. At the time of his presidency, he was rated as one of the most popular politicians in the history of Brazil and was respected around the world. As with others imprisoned for political activities under the military government, Lula was awarded a lifetime pension after the dictatorship fell, and before he was elected President.

Yes, anticipating and preparing for change is difficult. However, it is not so difficult when you understand and have an appreciation for comparative practices, not only between industries and competitors, but also between countries.

Today my prior company, as the merged Case New Holland, continues to maintain its manufacturing capabilities in Curitiba, Brazil. The company recently observed the 40th anniversary of establishing operations there.

If We Do as You Recommend, We Will Go to Jail

Usually, ethical relationships and definitions change over a period of time. For instance, in South Africa, apartheid was legally required, and at least the white citizens considered the legal requirement of apartheid as ethical. However, most of the rest of the world had moved toward a position in which discrimination based on color and separateness was inherently unethical.

For more than twenty-five years, apartheid was a festering issue around the world. During the 1960s, there were growing attacks on apartheid at the United Nations. Even so, in 1961, the year South Africa left the Commonwealth of Nations, a new constitution fully incorporated apartheid as a requirement.

At the same time, the U.S. was already preoccupied with its own civil rights movement, especially those efforts led by the Reverend Martin Luther King, Jr. Supporters of South Africans' efforts to overcome apartheid carefully watched the developments in the United States but were continually discouraged by the lack of democratic due process in South Africa. This was particularly true as it related to the opportunity to vote, and to limitations on black individuals' freedom to act and participate in basic legal protections.

My first major involvement with South Africa occurred when I was made the vice president for personnel relations for Sperry Corporation, a headquarters' position in New York City. Given this responsibility, I was anxious to meet the Sperry personnel director from South Africa, Colin Christy.

The United States corporate presence in South Africa became an important issue for the board of directors of especially those larger corporations doing business in South Africa. At annual shareholders' meetings, various interest groups regularly submitted shareholder proposals to the board about apartheid, including recommendations that the corporation leave South Africa in protest.

During the tenure of President Carter and U.S. Ambassador to the United Nations Andrew Young, the relationship between the United States and South Africa deteriorated. It was also during this period in 1977 that Leon Sullivan, a Baptist minister from Philadelphia, established the "Sullivan Principles."

Sullivan was a long-standing civil rights leader, and in 1971 was appointed as the first black member of the General Motors board of directors. Soon after being appointed to the board, he surprised fellow GM directors by suggesting General Motors should divest itself of GM's operations in South Africa in protest of apartheid. Although he was unsuccessful in getting GM to depart South Africa, his interest and insistence encouraged GM to adopt a human resource policy toward meaningful change in GM's South African operations. Compared with today's standards, the original principles, named after Reverend Sullivan, were very modest (for example, equal pay, integration of cafeterias and restrooms).

Eleven other firms joined General Motors as the original corporations pledging to follow the Sullivan Principles. By the mid-1980s, the list grew to 170 companies, including the Sperry Corporation. The participating companies' programs and progress were evaluated annually by the consulting firm Arthur D. Little.

It was in that setting that my discussions with the Sperry HR director from South Africa were held.

The problem, of course, was that we were dealing with an issue that was being treated quite differently between our two countries. At the same time, forecasting the future of this issue was not too difficult. With the South African white population possessing but a small percentage of the total country population, eventually the dominant black population would prevail. We did not know exactly when, but we knew we had to start to change our practices that day.

Colin and I agreed that we would present recommendations to the Sperry South African management to take corrective actions. Some South African management representatives suggested we would technically violate the existing apartheid law and "could be sent to jail."

In defense, we relied on two assumptions.

The first, and most important, was that apartheid was fundamentally unfair and by moral standards also unethical in almost all countries.

Second, from a practical standpoint, the government of South Africa was unlikely to impose sanctions against a major United States company that took such actions within its own company.

We did it. The accountable government officials blinked, or at a minimum, simply allowed us to go our own way. This was several years prior to the release of Nelson Mandela from prison in 1990. History proved that we had done the right thing.

The Widow's Benefit

In the mid-1980s, when I was a Sperry corporate vice president with responsibilities for worldwide compensation and benefits, I experienced another good example of the failure to anticipate change, especially in a global setting.

Most of the Sperry divisions had a major presence in the United Kingdom (UK). For a significant period of time, these units had been working on a revision of the corporate UK employee pension plan. They had a number of recommended changes and improvements. They submitted their revised pension plan for approval to the corporate headquarters in New York City. My job was to review their recommendations and provide input to the senior management that would be accountable for the final approval of the plan.

I had no problem with their recommendations until I saw a provision for a "Widows Benefit." This was to be a company-sponsored benefit and not linked to any governmental social security type of benefit.

I was ready to suggest they rename the benefit to a "survivor benefit." However, after reviewing the details of this benefit, to my surprise and disappointment, the benefit was to be applied only to male employees. Female employees would not have this benefit for their spouse.

As I questioned my UK friends about this obviously discriminatory benefit, they went on the defense. They highlighted that this was the nature of the benefit in the UK. They shared survey data verifying that some companies provided such a benefit in the manner that they were recommending. For good measure, they reminded me the plan was for the United Kingdom and not the United States. The muttered suggestion was the United States was preoccupied with equal employment opportunity-related issues.

In addition to challenging their proposal, I reminded them that in our UK subsidiaries, many women were highly placed in management, engineering, and other positions. Surely, I warned, they would see such a benefit as inherently discriminatory and unfair. The British management, however, argued that at that time the UK laws did not preclude such a benefit and, again, other companies they surveyed had such a plan.

They also argued that they had been working on this plan for longer than one year, and at no time during that period did anyone raise the concern I was raising about the Widows Benefit not applying to women. I asked how many women were on the committee drafting the recommendations. The answer was none.

I also argued that even if such a benefit was technically not illegal in the United Kingdom, surely the UK would be noting changing conditions around the world, including the United States, the home of our corporation. Why, I argued, should they, and the corporation, risk negative employee feedback, when future UK legislative changes would likely forbid this type of discriminatory benefit as well? Therefore, why not do it now, voluntarily? I also stressed that by extending the survivor benefit to women, the cost would not be significantly greater given the fact that women usually live longer than men and would be more likely to reach retirement age than men, at which time the benefit would expire.

All of this was for naught, however.

I reported the results of my review to my senior vice president who, in turn, was preparing to seek approval of the top senior management. I had no changes to the plan other than to suggest that the Widows Benefit be changed to a spouse's benefit. There was no support for my recommendation. It was met with the standard rationalization that, after all, "it is their country."

I arrived at the office early on the day the program was announced in the UK. As soon as I got to my office, I was told that UK officials were attempting to contact me. I returned their call immediately.

They informed me that they were having a "riot" by the female employees. They requested approval to include women in the Widows Benefit, to be renamed the Spouse's Benefit (or Survivor's Benefit). In addition, they were planning on telling everyone that they had always intended to include women and that the absence of the reference to women being entitled to this new benefit was an unfortunate "misprint."

My good UK friends learned a lesson in decision-making, as did my boss. With a smile on my face, I told them to go ahead.

CHAPTER 15

When You Discover Something Is Just Not Right, What Do You Do?

To perform satisfactorily a person must be intelligent, be reasonably educated, be knowledgeable, perform ethically, and have a keen interest in whatever he or she is doing.

To excel and provide leadership to others, there are two other major requirements: effort and dedication to what is right.

There is also a major difference between having the ability to do what you are told to do and leading.

Leading is developing an idea or direction that others have not considered or experienced and then promoting change. It is hard work. Leading requires significant initiative and effort. To lead effectively, an individual must be right many more times than wrong. On rare occasions, when a leader has made a poor decision, he or she must have the ability to recognize the error quickly and implement corrective action even faster than the original decision was made.

To be competent and not lead is wasting talent, or worse, being simply lazy.

To challenge the status quo is the best use of leadership skills and efforts. Fortunately, such leadership skills can be sometimes exercised and tested on the simplest of issues and challenges. Many of the examples throughout this book are that type.

The major challenge, organizationally and personally, is to advance a position that is so sensitive that others wish to avoid the issue. This is especially true when the issue affects management's rights and privileges.

Executive Medical—Round One

For me, it was an interest to do what was right that provoked me to attempt to change a simple, rather hidden, policy that benefited only the very top executives. However, it is the decisions on such issues that contribute to or detract from the organizations' culture.

Being an advocate for a position, such as someone's holiday pay, is relatively simple and usually low risk for the advocate. The real peril is when the advocate challenges something that threatens or disadvantages the boss and other key members of management.

There were numerous policies and practices I felt necessary to appeal, but the issue of my employer's policy for a special medical program for top executives was the most serious, risky, and lengthy appeal.

The issue was the executive medical plan. The story is this:

In the early 1980s, employers were becoming very concerned about the rising cost of health care benefits. Sperry Corporation had a special problem because it had so many diversified divisions ranging from retail products (Remington electric razors), to Sperry Flight Systems, Sperry Gyro/Defense Systems, Univac computers, Vickers hydraulics, and even farm equipment (New

Holland). Much earlier, Sperry took action to rationalize the various retirement programs and came up with one basic plan.

I was transferred from the New Holland division to the corporate staff in New York City with the primary objective of rationalizing and developing one health care program for the entire corporation.

In many companies, health care benefits plan designs did not promote cost-effectiveness or employee participation in cost-containment efforts. For instance, it was common for the health care benefits to be provided to employees at no cost whatsoever. Benefits were also very generous, such as 360 days of fully paid hospital benefits.

Other leading companies had already taken action to implement employee contributions, preferred provider networks, deductibles, and other health care design features encouraging employees to better manage health care costs.

After a lot of effort, we were successful in designing a new approach. Notwithstanding the higher level of cost borne by employees, we maintained a comprehensive program, and there was a reasonable level of acceptance. Employees understood that other companies were making similar changes. As we got ready to roll out the program, I considered having our chairman, Gerald Probst, possibly appear in a video on the importance of health care cost containment.

We also needed to prepare for future negotiations with the many bargaining units within Sperry. Having unions cooperate in the corporation's health care cost-containment efforts would benefit the company. However, their health care programs were subject to contractual negotiations.

The chairman of the company and a select few senior management officials had an executive health care program. Recipients of this "perk" included corporate officers, division presidents, and a small group of other very senior management. Under this program, they had no contributions, deductibles, or any other out-of-pocket expenses. It was a two-tier plan. The first provision was to have the members of senior management, and their qualifying family members, participate in the company's regular self-insured health care program. However, all executives' out-of-pocket costs, such as contributions, deductibles, co-payments, and other costs greater than the primary benefit, were reimbursed by a separate nonqualified plan.

This program existed for a number of years. However, because the prior regular employee programs were so generous and reimbursement levels so high, there was not much of a need for this executive program. This would change, however, given the intended recommendations to pass on more of the plan costs to employees. Left unattended, the executive plan would protect the executives from experiencing and participating in the same cost-reduction efforts planned for employees. The executives' basic program would also be reduced, but then their executive plan would reinstate them to a no out-of-pocket cost situation.

Given the additional concessions we were asking the employees to make, plus fully anticipating a difficult union negotiation environment, I was not anxious to defend the "company pay all" executive medical plan.

I, therefore, recommended to my boss, the senior VP, that the executive medical plan be discontinued. My strongest argument was that such a plan could not be justified by competitive conditions. Only about 15 percent of major companies had such an executive medical program. In addition, the trend was clearly downward with some plans being discontinued and none being implemented.

He did not like my recommendation one bit and aggressively argued how he had earned that benefit for himself through his long years of service. In addition, he reminded me that each of the participating officials in the executive medical plan had individual contracts with the corporation ensuring them that under no circumstances could the executive medical plan be discontinued.

I knew about the individual agreements so, at the same time, I recommended that we explain the problem to the participating executives. In other words, what may become a much more conspicuous and sensitive executive perk may cause a problem for not only the corporation, but for them as well.

True, we could not discontinue this perk unilaterally. However, we could ask the executives to surrender their rights to the plan and assist the corporation in gaining employee support for the new, less generous health and medical plan. To be fair, I also recommended that we offer some incentive to encourage the executives to discontinue participation under the plan.

I came up with an idea that we would offer those executives a special stock option if they discontinued their participation in the plan. In addition, I argued, if employee contributions, higher deductibles, and other cost-reduction methods were necessary to change employee expectations and encourage them to be intelligent health care consumers, shouldn't these also apply to the senior management? Or were they saying that they, with compensation in the hundreds of thousands of dollars, if not millions, could not afford a $250 deductible?

Surely, senior management should also be concerned with the continuation of this privileged benefit when their subordinates would be burdened with additional costs not previously experienced. I argued, how could we ask Mr. Probst, for instance, to appear in a video trying to explain the problem of health care cost containment when he would not be affected by the changes?

Still, my boss argued that employees did not even know about this benefit. He was right; most employees did not know of this special executive benefit. The benefit was only mentioned obliquely in the corporation's annual proxy statement.

I argued that we should not be influenced by the assumption that employees would remain unaware of this continuing executive perk. I argued we should do what was right. What was right was to discontinue the plan.

When it was obvious I could not get my boss to agree, I did something I have never done before. I asked my boss if I could appeal his decision and talk to Mr. Probst, the chairman, personally. I was asking permission to go "over his head." To his credit, he agreed I could do so.

My meeting with Probst was brief. I explained my recommendation, and he understood immediately. He agreed that he would approve discontinuing the executive medical plan to whatever extent that we could encourage participating executives to give up their "rights" to the plan by accepting some other more appropriate benefit.

Purposefully, I had not included in my recommendation what the quid quo pro would be. I wanted the issue of the executive medical plan to stand alone. However, I had already decided what I would recommend.

To assist, I engaged a consultant and then suggested the alternative I preferred. The consultant agreed that if the company had not implemented the executive medical plan years earlier, it would be difficult, under the current circumstances, to now justify establishing such a plan.

I included a consultant in the process not only to satisfy the professional requirement that my proposal was appropriate, but also to counter those company executives—as well as other HR directors—who felt the executive medical issue was only a "Losey" issue.

What we developed as the tradeoff instrument was restricted stock.

Unlike a typical stock option, restricted stock was essentially a gift after satisfying even a modest requirement, such as remaining with the company a certain period of time or meeting other objectives. This differs from a regular stock option that offers the opportunity for the manager or executive to purchase company stock at a future date based on the value/price of the stock on the day the option was granted. The intention with this type of regular stock option is to encourage all managers to dedicate their efforts to improve company performance, especially financial results, and that would normally help increase the price of the stock.

Another major difference with restricted stock is that a restricted stock grant is more like cash. Once the objective is met, the executive receives the restricted stock at no cost. Thus, again, unlike a regular stock option in which any gain is determined by subtracting the cost of the option, for instance, $75 a share, from the subsequent price at the time the option is exercised, for instance, $100. The gain is $25 and subject to taxation if exercised at the $100 price.

The restricted stock is valued at the time it matures and any performance or retention requirements are met. Since the restricted stock is essentially a gift, with no cost to the executive, it is taxed immediately, like cash.

The key point was this: Does the executive retain the executive medical plan but risk never needing it, or take the restricted stock that had a clearly defined benefit and almost immediate vesting?

Even if a few executives refused to turn in their executive medical plan for the restricted stock, the discontinuation of the plan would silence possible critics and reinforce that the company was trying to do the right thing.

I presented my boss with this approach and indicated I was ready to review my proposal with Mr. Probst, if my boss approved my proposal. My boss suggested that he, not me, would meet with Mr. Probst, presumably on my behalf.

After the meeting with Mr. Probst, my boss informed me that Mr. Probst approved the discontinuation of the executive medical plan. However, apparently my boss had added his own recommendation, which was to discontinue the plan for new entrants but "grandfather" the plan for the existing participants.

I was disappointed, but at least I could, if challenged, add that the plan had been discontinued and would eventually close when all participants expired.

Round Two

Not long after, however, there was a major reorganization with Joe Kroger, president of Univac, becoming the CEO of Sperry, reporting to Mr. Probst, the chairman.

Kroger immediately promoted a number of his former Univac subordinates to corporate level positions. At the same time, it was also decided to move the corporate headquarters from New York City to Blue Bell, Pennsylvania, the location of the Univac headquarters. My boss retired, and Kroger's HR person replaced him as corporate senior HR vice president.

I did then what I did for my next four HR corporate vice president bosses I worked for in as many years. My recommendation to them was what I would have done: volunteer to not participate in the executive medical plan. I advised that this would avoid the conflict of their participation in such a health care perk while also being responsible for designing and maintaining the health plans for employees,

Each refused to opt out of the plan with one suggesting he was not the "martyr" I was.

The Merger

Soon thereafter, the merger of Sperry with Burroughs occurred. Again, I was given the responsibility to now repeat the exercise I had done for Sperry—consolidate all the Burroughs and Sperry health and medical plans into one plan, plus do the same for all other employee benefits ranging from holidays to vacations, disability pay, retirement and savings plans, and more.

The objective was to come up with one competitive plan for the new Unisys Corporation, at no greater cost then the pre-merger cost. This meant many changes for employees from both prior companies. It took months and a lot of education, supportive communications, and compromises. Nevertheless, we did it.

When I presented the plan to my new boss, he approved it and mentioned it to Mr. Blumenthal, who summoned me to his conference room to review the planned changes with him.

Within minutes, I was in the conference room. He was pacing back and forth, not impatiently, but obviously interested in what the plan was before it went to the new Unisys board of directors. Yes, we all anticipated keen employee interest in such changes, and there were hundreds of millions of dollars involved.

He preempted my orderly review by shooting questions at me, which was his style. I answered them but finally suggested to him that if he sat down, I could, in a more orderly way, review the whole program. He sat down. My review took almost a half hour. He asked no other questions. When I finished, he told my boss that he did not want him to cover this subject with the board of directors but instead he wanted me to do it, presumably in the same rapid-fire fashion.

I also had the opportunity to broach the subject of executive medical plans being provided by both Sperry and Burroughs. I had received no permission to discuss this issue with Blumenthal and merely suggested the lack of merit in continuing those plans, and presumably any new Unisys executive medical plan. I told him I personally would recommend that we capture the current reorganization environment to discontinue this type of benefit. Given the type of equalitarian person Blumenthal was, he told me he would consider the discontinuation of the executive medical plan if that were part of the final recommendations. Unfortunately, I was unable to gain sufficient support among the key management to support that recommendation.

The Board

It was my first time in front of the total, new Unisys board. A few board members had been on the Sperry Board, but most, including the Unisys executives on the board, were from Burroughs.

Blumenthal gave me about twenty-five minutes to cover everything. I finished on time. A former Burroughs board member, at the time the chair of Warner-Lambert, obviously liked the presentation, volunteering that I "should be in sales."

Others were also very supportive. It was obvious the plan was going to be approved. There was only one issue that needed to be decided at this, the highest level. I favored that the company match in the 401(k) plan follow the employee's investment election. That was Sperry's policy. Given the retirement orientation of this benefit, Sperry management always felt matching in company stock, especially given the volatility of its industry, should not be the company match, unless, that was the employee's choice.

For Burroughs, however, the employer match had always been in the company's stock.

I raised this issue and was preempted by Jim Unruh, the CFO, who favored the former Burroughs approach. He also argued that there may be some financial benefits to the company by providing the company match in stock. Another advantage of using company stock for the match was it would result in the purchase of Unisys stock for the employees' match. This, in turn, might contribute to the demand for the stock and favorably influence the price.

Unruh won.

We did add a provision that allowed employees fifty years of age or older to change the match to go into whatever their investment election was.

Shortly thereafter, when the Unisys planned success story started to unravel, the stock started to decrease in value, disadvantaging the employees' matching accounts.

It was not until the Pension Protection Act of 2006 was enacted that the Unruh/Losey debate about how the company match should be invested was settled. The law changed, discontinuing the employer's opportunity to insist the employer match be in company stock. Furthermore, at least three materially different alternative investment options must be made available under these new guidelines. I have always regretted the obvious management delinquency when a law is passed requiring employers to do something that they should have done voluntarily.

As already highlighted, the failure of employers to anticipate the problems associated with racial and gender discrimination within the workplace was a major delinquency. Failure to provide safe working conditions resulted in the Occupational Safety and Health Act (OSHA). Failure to treat employees satisfactorily got employers the National Labor Relations Act, and union misconduct got the unions the Taft Hartley Act. The Employee Retirement Income Security Act (ERISA) was passed to ensure benefit programs voluntarily initiated for employees by employers, once established, provided protections from certain employer practices. And the list goes on.

By the time the Pension Protection Act of 2006 was passed, I was CEO at the Society for Human Resource Management (SHRM). I remember informing Unruh, by then the Unisys CEO, of the change in the law forbidding employers to insist that their 401(k) match be in company stock. I reminded him of the debate we had in front of the board on this issue. His response surprised and disappointed me. He said he did not recall the discussion or even the issue. Yet that decision touched many employee lives in a very negative way.

In my final days at Unisys, it was becoming increasingly clear to me that my management future within the company was limited, if not threatened. For instance, although I was responsible for all employee benefits planning and administration, given my well-known position on the executive medical plan, its administration was transferred to a peer of mine, who was far more accommodating. The plan was safe with him.

Round Three—Time To Leave

One day, I learned that God was an HR person. I received a call inquiring as to whether I would be interested in the position of president and CEO of SHRM.

Representatives of the SHRM board of directors interviewed me. I was offered and accepted their CEO position at essentially the same level of base compensation I had at Unisys. My major interest in the job was to concentrate more on the human resource management profession. Any compensation improvement was dependent on my performance and related bonus opportunity.

My last day at Unisys was preoccupied with filling boxes with the personal items I collected from my twenty-seven years at Sperry and the new Unisys service. Just before I walked out the door for the last time, I tried to see Jim Unruh, now the Unisys chairman. I wanted to express my appreciation for my long-standing employment. I also wanted to suggest that, as the new chair replacing Blumenthal, he could capture the opportunity to discontinue the executive medical program. He was not available, so I put my recommendation in writing (see next page). I left knowing my recommendation was registered one final time.

I never received a response.

UNISYS

Interoffice Memorandum

To: J. A. Unruh

Department: President & CEO

From: M. R. Losey .

Department: Human Resources

Subject: **AS I LEAVE...**

Date: October 12, 1990

Location: Blue Bell - A-1

Telephone: 423-5969

Location: Blue Bell - C2-NE5

cc:

As I leave... I wish to make one final appeal on the Executive Medical subject.

When I last discussed this subject with Curt Hessler, he suggested that he agreed with my position, but "I was talking to the wrong person" implying that you would be the final determiner of this issue. However, when you, Tom McKinnon, Curt, myself and others met to finalize the 1991 benefit initiatives, the issue did not surface. Following your example of assuming "ownership", I simply cannot leave without ensuring that you have had the opportunity to focus on this issue. You will note that I have not copied in Tom or Curt. You need not mention my appeal, of course. It's in your hands....

BACKGROUND

It was easier to defend Executive Medical when former Burroughs had 100% medical coverage and charged employees nothing for employees or dependents and when Sperry charged only $2.25 a month for dependent coverage. You more than most, appreciate how aggressively we have cut our health care program. Today, employees who sweep the floor are being charged up to $139.00 monthly for family coverage. In addition, we have implemented a Preferred Provider system, pre-certification, related penalties and are preparing to decrease the co-payment in 1991 from 85% to 80%. You will recall, Curt Hessler's closing comment as we made that difficult decision ..."we will need to make it someday, we might as well make it now". I agree with Curt, but if such a comment applies to our co-insurance rate, certainly it applies to the demise of Executive Medical.

Here is a summary of reasons that have been used to defend Executive Medical in the past:

"EMPLOYEES/STOCKHOLDERS DON'T KNOW ABOUT IT"

Executive Medical is fully disclosed in the Proxy statement. I have had the issue come up in collective bargaining sessions and heard many employees complain, especially secretaries of executives who benefit from this provision. Even if it is not widely known, equity cannot be advanced or defended by secrecy. Also, the longer the benefit continues and the wider the treatment gap grows, the greater the potential employee relations impact will be when it is fully discovered/disclosed.

J. A. Unruh
October 12, 1990
Page Two

Certainly the benefit is widely known amongst HR professionals. It compromises their position as they are asked to defend company initiatives in the healthcare area as well as our collective bargaining position. It also contradicts leading management practice which suggests that executives can best set an example by paying the premiums and absorbing deductibles, co-payments, etc. at least as aggressive as the standard employee plans, if not greater.

Finally, discontinuing Executive Medical would overcome the objection we had from several HR directors recently when we wanted to have you address employees (on a video) about healthcare cost containment. This suggestion was vetoed by the field in part because of your personal entitlement to Executive Medical. HR executives felt that as long as you and other executives have this benefit, you cannot credibly speak to the issue of the seriousness of healthcare costs to the company.

"SIMPLICITY FOR EXECUTIVES"

Another defense has been that we do not wish to burden executives with the calculation of deductibles, co-payments and other related requirements. Such a position is preposterous. At the very least, executives should pay the required premiums for coverage.

"THE PROGRAM IS A COMPETITIVE PRACTICE CUSTOMARILY EXTENDED TO EXECUTIVES"

The program is NOT A COMPETITIVE PRACTICE. Only 15% of the top 100 firms in the United States continue to maintain Executive Medical programs. Any executive or HR professional who maintains otherwise does not do his homework. I could never suggest to management or the Board that employees be extended a benefit simply because 15% of other companies have such a provision.

"THE COMPETITIVE PRECEDENT, ALTHOUGH MINIMAL, IS NOT DECREASING"

Once I convince others that few companies have Executive Medical, the retort is those that do have the benefit are not eliminating it. This statement is also incorrect. In 1988, 17% of the top 100 companies had Executive Medical, again, this has now decreased to 15%. One can also anticipate that when a precedent exists with so few companies there is a risk that such companies are indifferent to the normal sanctions associated with continuing this benefit. Surely Unisys, with our renewed emphasis on equality of sacrifice and building of corporate culture, should not default to this group.

J. A. Unruh
October 12, 1990
Page Three

"IT DOESN'T COST THAT MUCH"

Admittedly, the cost to provide Executive Medical is not great -- estimated to be less than $2,500 per year per qualifying executive. I ask, therefore, why we continue to aggressively defend Executive Medical if it is such a small benefit, especially when the consequences associated with highlighting disparate treatment are so great.

"IT'S NOT THE RIGHT TIME"

Some argue that executives have been disproportionately burdened with the down-turn in business conditions, especially in regards to bonuses, and additional benefit "cut backs" would not be appropriate at this time. I argue that now is the best time.

Although I have reason to believe that Mr. Blumenthal shared my sympathy for eliminating Executive Medical, your recent appointment to the Presidency offers an excellent opportunity to change this policy. You could be viewed as more equalitarian and would also set a standard for other executives. It will reinforce the important concept of equality of sacrifice and treatment.

"THIS IS A 'LOSEY' ISSUE; OTHERS IN HR DO NOT FEEL AS STRONGLY"

Several have suggested that I have come close to losing perspective on this issue and that Executive Medical has become my personal vendetta. My response is that I have been willing to go to extraordinary efforts and assume the necessary risks if I feel something is inequitable -- I feel this way about Executive Medical. In addition, I suggest I have more knowledge and skill than the average HR individual, many of whom still believe that the program is competitively justified or are not willing to risk the wrath of management by suggesting its demise.

Finally, I am continually astonished as to how people, for instance, brought in from IBM -- which would under no circumstances entertain such a benefit -- now accept it freely and take every action to defend it. Where is their "ownership"? This is all the more reason why the standard must come from the top. Thus, my final appeal to you... as I leave.

Jim, good luck. I know you have a thankless job. As you may have heard, however, as I leave I am trying to build encouragement that Unisys can and will make it.

I wish you, Tom McKinnon, Curt Hessler and my many other friends at Unisys continued best wishes. If I can be of any assistance in the future, please do not hesitate to call upon me.

M. R. Losey

MRL:pal

At SHRM

Given the poor Unisys performance, bonuses were negatively affected. However, if I turned the SHRM performance around and made meaningful improvements, the opportunity for increasing my overall compensation was substantial.

At the end of our first year, we had increased membership and improved our financial results, allowing us to contribute a record $1 million-plus to net asset reserves (profit in the for-profit sector.)

When I retired nine years later, membership had grown more than 300 percent, and net assets more than 900 percent.

Round Four—Discontinuing the Executive Medical Plan

In the meantime, the Unisys story got worse. Difficult times required an assortment of corrective actions, many of which affected employees. First, there were the layoffs, which came one after the other. As is customary in such situations, every effort was taken to reduce costs.

One action dealt with retirees. Unisys discontinued a very popular benefit: post-retirement medical.[31] This action affected more than 25,000 former employees, now retirees. Employees and retirees brought several major class-action lawsuits that sought to reverse the termination of the retirees' health care plan. Many suggested they had been promised post-retirement medical for life.

Although I had been gone from Unisys for several years, Unisys asked if I would assist in its defense, given the fact I was the one who helped design not only the new Unisys benefits program but also the previously revised benefits program for

---

31 Actually, "post-retirement medical" is a misnomer. Post-retirement is death. Providing health insurance to employees who retired should have been characterized as "post-employment."

the former divisions of Sperry Corporation. Nor, I suspect, did Unisys hesitate to use me as an expert, given that I was then the president and CEO of SHRM, the largest human resource management professional society in the world.

The key issue was, did Unisys reserve the right to make unilateral changes to its benefits plans? This is referred to as a "reservation of rights" clause in any employee benefits plan. I could testify that this was not only a standard policy within companies, but more specifically, was intentionally included in the Unisys plans.

In addition, although Unisys was one of the first to do so, other companies were examining their retiree benefits policies out of concern about increasing medical costs for a growing population of retirees. They, too, were making changes that included discontinuing their plans.

I testified that Unisys had, indeed, reserved the right to make unilateral changes to the retirees' plans. The changes were consistent with the plans' provisions. I had to tell the truth. I felt terrible that difficult post-merger business conditions required major restructuring and cost reduction. Now, included in the cost reduction was the retirees losing their post-retirement benefit.

I was curious, however, as to whether the company—in its horrible business climate—would finally take this opportunity to discontinue the executive medical plan. I thought that if it spent a lot of time considering whether it should discontinue retiree plans, surely the existence of the executive medical privileged benefit should have also been reviewed.

I wrote to the secretary of the corporation, Bobette Jones,[32] asking if there were any plans to discontinue the executive

---

32 A corporate officer customarily used for shareholder questions.

medical program. Although I did not expect her to divulge any confidential information, I reinforced the general impression by many that it was becoming increasingly difficult to justify this extremely generous benefit given Unisys's overall business condition and what it had done to retirees.

Her weak argument was that this benefit was needed to retain key executives. I challenged her asking how this could be the case given that approximately 85 percent of comparable companies did not offer such a plan. I told her I would be sending her something more on this issue, and I sent her a shareholder proposal recommending that the Unisys executive medical plan be discontinued.

I complied with the statutory requirements for such a shareholder proposal, such as owning sufficient shares of stock, holding the shares until the planned annual meeting, and limiting my shareholder proposal to five hundred words or less. There was also the prohibition of submitting a shareholder proposal that preempts management's right to determine employee terms and conditions, such as how many holidays to provide or granting a pay increase.

To further advance my right to submit a shareholder proposal related to Unisys executives' perks, I stated that Unisys employees were the largest single shareholder as a result of the Unisys 401(k) plan. I argued they had the right to know the specifics and decide for themselves if the Unisys executive medical plan was appropriate.

I also provided copies of my shareholder proposal to Jim Unruh, president and CEO, and I crafted special appeals to several Unisys board members I knew personally.

I did not have to wait long for an answer. I suspect it was only one or two days after everyone had received my shareholder proposal. Tom McKinnon, the senior vice president for human resources, was given the task of informing me, verbally, that Unisys was going to discontinue the executive medical plan.

Because I had previously pledged to withdraw my shareholder proposal if Unisys discontinued the plan, I immediately withdrew it.

I do not know how many shareholder proposals had been submitted to a corporation that resulted in the board of directors accepting the recommendation of the shareholder(s). The Manhattan Institute for Policy Research reported that in 2014,[33] even after gaining a position on a proxy ballot, only 4 percent of the proposals were supported by a majority of shareholders. How many shareholder proposals a board of directors approved voluntarily is unknown, but presumed to be minuscule.

33 Stephen Joyce, "N.Y. Official Boosts Shareholder Proposals in 2015," Manhattan Institute for Policy Research, September 29, 2015, http://www.proxymonitor.org/forms/shareholder_proposals_sj.aspx.

CHAPTER 16

What Would You Do If You Were the CEO?

Early in my career, the following incident affected my approach to management and leadership more than almost anything else.

It was the first meeting I attended, which was run by George Delp, the chairman of our New Holland division. As the lowest-ranking person in the room, I was not sitting at the long conference table but instead back against the wall, with my participation limited to observing, I thought.

I was paying attention and enjoyed hearing Delp quiz the different department heads and observing the debates between the executives.

Then, rather abruptly, Delp turned and asked me what I thought we should do on the subject the group was discussing.

I answered immediately. "Who me? I am in personnel!" It was probably the dumbest thing I said in my whole career.

From that day on, I did more than just listen to the discussion. I studied each issue and thought, "What would I do if I were the CEO of the company?"

Quite possibly a potential leader's lack of participation or presumed ignorance will contribute to an assumption about his or her performance, such as, "What the hell do you know?" New leaders should expect, but not allow, that presumption to discourage them from volunteering suggestions outside their area of responsibility.

Make that suggestion even at the risk of being conspicuously rejected or obliquely ignored. Then wait. See what happens. Did what you suggested develop, become true, or now more likely look like a good solution for the prior issue or problem?

If it does, then you are on the right track, and your confidence will improve. The next time you make a suggestion that is rejected, remind the rejecters of the negative consequences of others having not listened to their previous recommendations that were later shown to have merit.

On the other hand, if future developments prove the rejected proposal should have been vetoed, learn from the experience, try to do better next time, and by all means keep thinking, "What would I do if I were the CEO?"

At the same time, do not be disappointed if you do not become the CEO. Almost all the readers of this book will not become a CEO. For instance, what if an aspiring leader goes to work for General Motors that employs 215,000 employees or IBM with 375,000 employees? Does this ambitious leader have an expectation, or even remote hope, that he or she will end his or her career as the CEO? Probably not.

However, most people want to have a successful career and possibly be a respected leader. Unfortunately, there will always be a shortage of good leaders.

Potential leaders should never underestimate their capabilities.

Sue Meisinger was the vice president for governmental affairs when I became SHRM's CEO. I had known her earlier, and now I know that she was the person who recommended me as a possible SHRM CEO candidate.

After I joined SHRM, Sue reported to me in her government lobbyist role and supervised a number of other lobbyists. In department heads meetings, she was always prepared and reported skillfully and comprehensively about her department's activities. However, I noticed she was conspicuously quiet when other departments reported or raised issues. I suspected it was her reluctance to comment on other departments' issues.

Sue was a very high performer and a lawyer and was extremely bright, with excellent interpersonal skills. She had obvious potential. I told her I had one disappointment, and that was her lack of contribution in the department heads meetings. She seemed surprised, and as anticipated, offered she did not want to risk interjecting herself into other managers' responsibilities.

I told her she had only one problem: that she had no idea how good she was and how much she had to offer. I encouraged her to follow my principle of always considering, "What would I do if I were the CEO or the department head of a different department than my own?"

I reminded her that her reluctance to contribute or challenge others when she thought it necessary was not only detracting from her being a good team player but also increasing the probability that we might fail to select our best strategy, or worse, make a serious mistake. I followed this advice with giving her more responsibility for other departments. She was very successful in expanding her capabilities and reaching her full potential.

As it is well known, Sue was ultimately selected by the board of directors to become SHRM's president and CEO.

Completed Staff Work

I also learned from a former boss the importance of completed staff work. He would instruct me to answer some inquiry, study an issue, or write a memo for him on some subject. The objective was to bring the memo to him with an expectation that all he would have to do was sign it.

I must admit, initially, I became somewhat irritated. It seemed as if I was doing all the work, and he was getting all the credit. Then it occurred to me that this process was an opportunity. I moved from trying to anticipate what the boss might want to instead thinking about what I would do. I was, more frequently, not responding to his requests but, instead, offering initiatives I identified myself. It was great fun and yielded a rewarding sense of accomplishment when all he had to do was sign a document to advance my idea.

Within a year, I replaced my boss.

Yes, if you can advance your ideas through your boss, taking the lead will work much more effectively than merely "toting the boss's briefcase" (in other words, just being obedient and doing little more than what you are instructed to do). Taking the lead is the best way to illustrate your competency and potential leadership.

The Ninety-Five-Year-Old Retiree

To save money, the Unisys finance department strongly suggested that we discontinue the opportunity for retirees to elect a health management organization (HMO). I objected, suggesting that any financial savings would be very small, if any, and not worth the price of upsetting retirees during what was already a difficult post-merger period. I also reminded finance that communicating with retirees is challenging, usually resulting in the actual communication being primarily with the sons and daughters of the retirees. Some retirees were so old that many of the sons and daughters were also retired or soon-to-be retired.

The finance department did not accept my advice to retain this specific provision within the current post-retirement medical plan. Notwithstanding the rejection of my recommendation, finance asked me to review its plan and obtain the final approval of the department's proposed change from Mr. Blumenthal, the chairman of the company.

In our meeting, I explained the reasons why this change, excluding retirees from HMO participation, was being made. Mr. Blumenthal, who was getting ready to retire himself, immediately protested this change for reasons unrelated to his situation. In a loud voice, he said, "My father is retired and participates in Kaiser Permanente's HMO plan. If he lost his plan, he would be very upset." He continued briefly, given his command of the meeting, suggesting such a change was not worth it.

Mr. Blumenthal had concluded falsely that I was in favor of the change. Fortunately, my boss and the senior executives of finance came to my rescue, so that the messenger would not be killed. They made it very clear to Mr. Blumenthal that the viewpoint he had just shared exactly matched my own. Blumenthal thanked me for advancing finance's recommendation even though I did not support it. More importantly, he thanked me for my position since it was the same as his.

I had played the "What would I do if I were the CEO" game and won. Finance's recommendation was killed. It was one of the shortest meetings I ever attended.

Summer Jobs for Executives' Sons And Daughters

The top executives and officers of Burroughs previously had a summer employment program for their sons and daughters. It

survived the merger and was expanded to include the children
of the former Sperry executives who now qualified.

Under this program, the Unisys human resource department was expected to contact the qualifying executives' sons
and daughters and ask them where they wanted to work geo-
graphically. Based on their responses, the company developed
employment opportunities at those locations for the children of
the executives.

Mr. Blumenthal did not know of this program. One day,
he discovered its existence. He did not like it. His exact words
were, "Those kids have enough advantages. Give the summer
jobs to students who need them." This was his equalitarian side.

Many of the former Burroughs executives were not pleased
with the discontinuation of this program for their kids. They
complained to my boss. He told me he had a remedy for this
problem. What he proposed was that we take the lead and contact other major corporations, especially in the Philadelphia area
where our headquarters was located. He suggested we would
offer the executives' children of other area major corporations
summer employment opportunities within Unisys if they shared
opportunities within their own corporations for our executives'
children.

My boss told me to set up the program.

In addition to a rather substantial administrative burden
when we were in the middle of a merger, I objected to my boss
on the basis this plan would not only circumvent but violate
Mr. Blumenthal's intentions. I told my boss that I felt very
uncomfortable doing what he instructed me to do and would
prefer not to do it.

I am sure my boss did not appreciate my position, but he
said he understood. He abruptly ended the meeting without

additional comment. Soon thereafter, he employed the wife of one of the corporation's senior executives to coordinate this program.

My actions did not contribute much to my reputation for being a good "team player." That was okay.

CHAPTER 17

Business Ethics— Leaders' Responsibilities

"It would have been my preference to have more investigation of individual action, since obviously everything that went wrong or was illegal was done by some individual, not by an abstract firm."[34]

—BEN BERNANKE, FORMER FEDERAL RESERVE BANK CHAIR

Headlines highlighted the billions of dollarΩs in fines imposed on major banks and brokerage firms for their reckless lending and securities dealings that contributed greatly to the 2008 recession. However, was that enough?

Former Federal Reserve Chairman Ben Bernanke has made it very clear he did not think so. He suggested some Wall Street executives should have gone to jail for their misconduct.

---

34 Susan Page, "Ben Bernanke: More Execs Should Have Gone to Jail for Causing Great Recession," *USA Today*, October 5, 2015, http://www.usatoday.com/story/news/politics/2015/10/04/ben-bernanke-execs-jail-great-recession-federal-reserve/72959402/.

IMPACT

In my management teaching on ethics, I customarily start with asking the class what the best answer is to the following question:

"What can do the greatest harm to an organization?"
A. Competitor actions
B. Labor strike
C. Poor quality
D. Ethics violations

Any one of these answers could be the correct answer depending on the situation. For the right answer related to ethics violations, we need only examine the magnitude of the negative impact of what has happened to one of the foremost companies in the world—Volkswagen (VW). Possessing one of the finest reputations for innovation, quality, and performance, and for the first six months of 2016 passing Toyota as the world's top automaker, the management threatened it all with headlines about it cheating on emissions controls.

Less than a week after the Environmental Protection Agency ordered Volkswagen to recall nearly 500,000 vehicles that were equipped with software that tricked emissions tests, the company's CEO, Martin Winterkorn, announced he would resign although insisting he had no knowledge of these violations.[35]

In November 2016, Volkswagen announced plans to cut 30,000 jobs, or about 5 percent of its worldwide workforce, in a wide-ranging restructuring as it tries to recover from the scandal.[36]

---

35 https://consumerist.com/2015/09/23/volkswagen-ceo-resigns-amid-emissions-violation-scandal/.
36 http://www.observer-reporter.com/20161118/vw_to_shed_30000_jobs_cutting_costs_after_scandal.

The VW fiasco was avoidable by policy, procedures, and basic ethics. It does not take much knowledge about manufacturing to know that what was done at VW is impossible for an individual, alone, to do. The company's illegal emission-control software had to be designed, become a major component of the car, be given a part number, and be tested to ensure it worked as illegally intended. Furthermore, the company had to ensure replacement units were available, determine where to place the product within the car, build the unit, and install it.

All of these steps have various levels of required approval. Those employees and managers knew what this equipment was designed to do—provide an illegal and unethical product to avoid the emissions regulations. Surely, there were no exceptions to VW's policy to give them the authority to do what they did. How far up the management chain did this authorization of illegal activity go? One level, two, three, four? What happens to those who assumed the responsibility to add a capability for the VW cars to circumvent the laws and regulations of many countries and their dealers and customers' best interests?

What business culture allowed and apparently encouraged VW management representatives to risk the sanctions and negative impact on a reputation that took many, many years to establish?

All involved assumed the risk, despite knowing the probable horrible damage to the company's reputation and the tremendous financial impact of their misdeeds. That initial financial impact was stated to be $18 billion, as VW announced in April 2016, more than double the amount the company had previously set aside for pending technical modifications and customer-related measures as well as for global legal risks."[37]

In January 2017 the Volkswagen Group announced it "expects to reach a multibillion-dollar criminal and civil settlement with the U.S. Justice Department and U.S. Customs and Border Protection over its emissions scandal."[38]

Volkswagen also admitted it expects to plead guilty to criminal charges that the company engineered greater than half a million U.S. diesel vehicles with software to cheat emissions standards. It was estimated that the cost of any proposed settlement would be an additional $4.3 billion, or approximately $8,600 per violating vehicle.[39]

The impact on the company is enormous and will be longstanding. And it is not just the billions and billions VW will pay in fines and fixes. How much is a company and its German home-country reputation worth? In this instance, the ethics violations have caused much more damage to the company than any union demand or action, any quality issue, or competitor achievement could inflict. And they did it to themselves!

Even as members of the top management embarrassingly suggest they had no knowledge of these practices and, therefore, should be insulated from legal prosecution, the senior management will, nevertheless, pay a high price. Those leaders will feel the sorrow of not learning what they should have known, and of failing to establish a culture that either would

---

37 Nathan Bomey, "Cost of Volkswagen Emissions Scandal Balloons to $18B," *USA Today*, April 22, 2016, http://www.usatoday.com/story/money/cars/2016/04/22/volkswagen-emissions-scandal-cost/83379520/.

38 Nathan Bomey, "Volkswagen expects $4.3B criminal, civil settlement with feds, *USA Today*, January 11, 2017, page 3A

39 Ibid.

not permit such violations or, if violations occurred, would urge prompt reporting of inappropriate conduct.

Consistent with the theme of this book, what the VW executives will regret most is the personal negative impact on customers, shareholders, employees, dealers, communities, and even their nation. Negatively touching hundreds of thousands, if not millions, of lives will be the offenders' legacy.

Are You a Team Player?

As New Holland's vice president for human resources, I was at Sperry's headquarters in New York City attending a meeting of all the HR vice presidents from the various Sperry divisions. Frank Sweeten, the corporation's senior vice president for human resources, coordinated the meeting.

Customarily, we started the meeting with a roundtable discussion with each HR division head reporting on developments in his or her respective division.

The HR VP of Sperry's defense systems division, headquartered at Great Neck, New York, shared how proud its division was about a relationship with one of New York State's senators in Washington, D.C. He reported that his division had been working with one of its state senators to advance legislation that would be so specific in regard to the requirements and technology of planned new weaponry that the project would, constructively, leave Sperry as the sole bidder.

As heads nodded in agreement that the division's tactic was a clever approach, I was not so sure. I interrupted and asked whether it was appropriate for the corporation to try to influence legislation in such a way that it would compromise and disadvantage the government's bidding process.

You would have thought I had conspicuously farted in the conference room. I was quickly sanctioned, specifically by Mr. Sweeten, and without opposition from the others. More specifically it was suggested that I, from the corporation's farm equipment division, did not understand the defense business. "This is the way business is done in Washington," was the consensus. Again, I was hearing the "playground" excuse. In other words, if everyone else does it, it is okay for us to do it also.

They did not change my mind, but I shut up.

A few years later, I was promoted to be the corporation's vice president for compensation and benefits. Each year, at bonus time, I had to consolidate and review the executive bonus submissions from the various division presidents. In my review, one bonus stuck out as extraordinarily large. I brought this to the attention of my boss, now Frank Sweeten.

He reminded me that this bonus was for Charles Gardner, the executive from Great Neck who had the influential government contacts in Washington, D.C. Thus, Frank suggested the large bonus was justified.

Operation Ill Wind

As mentioned earlier, Unisys was formed in 1986 by the merger of mainframe computer manufacturers Sperry Corporation and Burroughs Corporation.

In the same year, 1986, several years after I raised these ethical issues, the U.S. Department of Justice (DOJ) started a three-year investigation of fraud in defense procurement, known as Operation Ill Wind. The investigation found that Unisys, the surviving company from the merger of Sperry and Burroughs, committed fraud and bribery in the process of obtaining defense contracts. The result was criminal convictions for more than a dozen Unisys (formerly Sperry) executives and consultants. Mr. Gardner led the list.

Six other companies, nine government officials, and forty-two individuals were prosecuted as a result of that investigation, with Unisys' fines and penalties totaling $190 million.[40]

I clearly remember being with Mr. Blumenthal, Unisys's chairman, when he expressed his disappointment that his newly created company, Unisys, would now be burdened with a $190 million fine and a major blow to the yet-to-be-fully-defined Unisys reputation.

Specifically, I recall him saying, "I learned the definition of vicarious liability." He highlighted that in English law, the doctrine of vicarious liability imposes liability on employers for the wrongdoings of their employees.[41] Therefore, when Mr. Blumenthal acquired Sperry, now part of Unisys, Unisys became liable for the illegal acts by Mr. Gardner and others.

The DOJ gave Mr. Gardner one of the severest sentences for his part in the fraud case. He was sentenced to thirty-two months in jail; plus, a $40,000 fine was imposed on him for the leadership role he played in bribing government officials.

As the L.A. Times reported, "A Gardner associate, James G. Neal, was sentenced to 27 months in prison and fined $30,000 for creating secret offshore accounts to bribe Pentagon officials and members of Congress to help Unisys win multibillion-dollar defense contracts.

---

40 Brooke Williams, "Windfalls of War: Unisys Corporation," Center for Public Integrity, n.d., http://web.archive.org/web/20071215105158/http://www.publicintegrity.org/wow/bio.aspx?act=pro&ddIC=59.

41 "Vicarious Liability in English Law," Wikipedia, https://en.wikipedia.org/wiki/Vicarious_liability_in_English_law.

Gardner, 58, admitted in March that he had directed Neal to bribe former Assistant Secretary of the Navy Melvyn R. Paisley by purchasing Paisley's ski resort condominium at an inflated price in return for preferential treatment on Navy and Marine Corps business.

At the same time, Neal admitted paying $400,000 to Garland L. Tomlin Jr., a former Navy engineer, to help Unisys win a large Navy contract. Tomlin is awaiting sentencing after pleading guilty to bribery charges earlier this year."[42]

Tomlin pleaded guilty to bribery charges and received an 18-month sentence.

At the earlier corporate meeting, I had been worried about what I was hearing and questioned a practice I thought was not ethical. The actions I had protested were initiated from this violating division. Yes, I had suffered the accusation I was not knowledgeable about such business practices, and it was implied I was not a "team player." This experience contributed to my "digging in" on workplace ethical issues. My advice to others is this: If, in a difficult situation, you are ever asked if you are a team player, look out. Such a challenge might be constructive admission that the decision or effort is short on supporting logic, policy, and regulatory compliance, and long on risk and negative consequences.

Enron and More

When Enron collapsed more than fifteen years ago, lawmakers and watchdog agencies wanted to more broadly examine issues such as securities fraud and accounting irregularities. Lawmak-

---

42 John M. Broder, "Ex-Unisys Official Is Sentenced in Bribery Case," *Los Angeles Times*, September, 16, 1989, http://articles.latimes.com/1989-09-16/business/fi-268_1_unisys-corp.

ers, and others, wanted to know how a presumably skillful and honest management could take or permit actions that so severely disadvantaged shareholders and employees.[43] However, then the bigger concern surfaced. That was whether Enron's situation was an isolated incident or evidence of systematic failure that might threaten the most basic requirement of our economic system: corporate credibility.[44]

Now that question seems to be answered. We still regularly see announcements of questionable management actions, and, in some cases, possibly illegal practices. These actions are taken by highly educated, well-positioned, networked, and generously compensated corporate executives.[45]

My first effort on editorializing about business ethics was more than fifteen years ago. Shareholders and employees of such companies as Global Crossing, Quest, Adelphia, ImClone Systems, WorldCom, and even Martha Stewart Living Omnimedia witnessed the crippling impact of a company without ethics. Surely, we thought, the message was out, and the consequences well defined. We had learned our lesson, I had hoped.

Wells Fargo—Founded March 1852

"The name Wells Fargo is forever linked with the image of a six-horse stagecoach thundering across the American West, loaded with gold. The full history, over more than 160 years, is rich in detail with great events in America's history. From the Gold Rush to the early 20th Century, through prosperity, depres-

---

43 Some information sourced from an original article by M. R. Losey for the American Society of Association Executives: "Free Enterprise Is Everyone's Responsibility," *Association Management*, October 2002, http://www.mikelosey.com/asae.htm.

44 Ibid.

45 Ibid.

sion and war, Wells Fargo earned a reputation of trust due to its attention and loyalty to customers."[46]

So much for Wells Fargo history and past efforts.

Now this bank is being fined $185 million. The reason? Because of its systematic and inappropriate signing up of two million customers for unauthorized accounts. Why? For some in Wells Fargo management, it seemed like a good idea at the time!

They apparently convinced themselves that this was the only way to meet what they considered were unreasonably high sales quotas. So they rationalized their justification, and adopted, for companywide use, this illegal conduct.

Now there is no place to hide.

Suggesting the company is taking aggressive action to promptly stop this illegal practice by terminating 5,300 employees falls way short. More than that, it is an insult to their customers, the public, and most of all, their own employees.

For instance, why did it take five years to stop an obvious inappropriate, illegal practice? That is a long time. How many employees were involved? 5,300! That is a long line of people. Two million customer accounts! A huge number.

How could those involved maintain any reasonable expectation that they would not be caught? With such enormous numbers, it was not a question of if they would get caught, but when.

These actions had to be obvious to many, many executives and employees. Why the silence?

The day I first saw this breaking news in *USA Today*, I wrote the chairman of the Wells Fargo board of directors. I was furious since these actions are exactly what I hate to see in our economic system.

I wrote the following letter expressing my displeasure:

46 "History of Wells Fargo," https://www.wellsfargo.com/about/corporate/history/.

MICHAEL R. LOSEY, SPHR, CAE
CEO, Noted Author, Speaker, Panelist, Expert Witness
and Global Human Resource Management Leader

2168 AUTUMN COVE CIRCLE, Fleming Island, FL 32003 • PHONE: 904-215-5316 • CELL: 904-613-0233 • E-MAIL: mlosey@mikelosey.com

September 10, 2016

> "Everything we do is built on trust. It doesn't happen with one transaction, in one day on the job or in one quarter. It's earned relationship by relationship."
>
> John G. Stumpf, Chairman and CEO

Corporate Offices
Wells Fargo
420 Montgomery Street
San Francisco, CA 94104

Dear Mr. Stumpf:

I am delivering this correspondence to your local bank branch, here is Fleming Island, FL and instructing them to close my Wells Fargo account.

I shall share with my local Wells Fargo representatives yesterday's USA Today article on how Wells Fargo has cheated millions of customers and will cost shareholders at least $185 million in fines, penalties and possible customer reimbursements.

The Wells Fargo comment that you have "terminated approximately 5300 employees and managers over a five-year period for their involvement with the accounts" magnifies the seriousness of this systemic fraud. In five years, why wasn't the problem clearly identified by Wells Fargo management and corrective action taken long ago?

How could you possibly allow this to happen?

What is the highest level of Wells Fargo management that has known and allowed these fraudulent actions to take place? Is it, you sir? If not, who then and are they still on the payroll?

Our nation was founded on a few very important principles: Individual freedom, religious freedom and the concept of free-enterprise. You are accountable for damaging the cornerstone of our free-enterprise system - Honesty.

I hand-delivered a copy of my Stumpf letter to a representative at my local Wells Fargo branch. I told her, given the bank's inappropriate actions, I wanted to close my account. The representative's conduct was very professional, and she closed my account without debate. As I was departing, I asked her how many other customers had closed their account.

Her answer: "None." Sadly, it did not surprise me. Customer indifference, not forgiveness, is the tragedy.

After continued massive negative feedback, Mr. Stumpf subsequently resigned with more than $100 million in vested entitlements.

Why the Indifference?

If business ethics is so important, then why do only government agencies investigate and attempt to correct what goes wrong within these types of unethical companies?

As highlighted in my letter to Stumpf, America's Founding Fathers, seeking new freedoms and a better way of life, fully supported the free-enterprise system that underpins more than our commerce—it is our way of life. However, such a free-enterprise system comes with a profound measure of personal responsibility. It is these violating companies, and their executives who violate their responsibility, that hurt all of us.

Many of these executives—such as Enron's CEO, Jeffrey Skilling; WorldCom's CEO, Bernard Ebbers; ImClone's chair, Sam Waskal; Adelphia's founder, John Rigas; and Tyco's CEO, Dennis Kozlowski—went to jail.

Why did they do what they did?

Ex-Tyco chief Dennis Kozlowski may have summed it up for many wayward executives when he admitted he took millions from the corporation he governed because he "fell into what I can best describe as a CEO bubble, and I rationalized that I was more valuable than I was."[47]

Most of these executives had been highly involved in their corporations for years—surely sufficient time to thoroughly understand the strengths and weaknesses of their enterprise. Why were there no earlier warnings from the top?

And, if such leaders could not, or did not want to, blow the whistle, what about their key financial staff members? Could they not fathom their employers' problems and possible violations? Or, as we witnessed in some cases, were they also part of the problem?

In Enron's case, Arthur Andersen, its outside auditing firm, waited too long to notify the Enron board of directors of possible illegal acts. That delinquency in performance cost Arthur Andersen dearly. In 2002, the firm voluntarily surrendered its licenses to practice as certified public accountants. The company escaped a very close call when the United States Supreme Court set aside the guilty judgment of criminal charges relating to its handling of Enron's books. However, by that time the damage had been done. Other national accounting and consulting firms bought some of the practices of Arthur Andersen. The devastation to its reputation has prevented Arthur Andersen from returning to its former reputation and dominance in the industry.

Even if the external auditors dropped the ball, what about the company's board of directors? Where was its oversight? It has an absolute fiduciary responsibility to shareholders, and, in my opinion, to our free-enterprise system.

If we cannot depend on highly placed people, what about other employees who dealt with accounts payable and receiv-

---

47 http://www.huffingtonpost.com/2013/12/03/convicted-ex-tyco-ceo-kozlowski_n_4380263.html

ables, reviewed sales reports, and saw what was delivered and what wasn't? Didn't anyone notice that something was wrong? Is not the silent employee just as responsible as the defrauding executive?

Outside the company, what about those highly paid, cuff-linked executives from Wall Street who can predict the company's earnings per share almost to the penny? Where were they when we really needed them?[48]

The financial press also let us down. A short time prior to Enron's collapse, *Money* magazine published the disastrous Enron buy recommendation of Janus fund manager Blaine Rollins. As Enron's largest shareholder, did Janus really believe that Enron was "still posting 20-30 percent earnings growth," as Rollins told *Money* only days before everything collapsed?[49]

As I wrote in a 2002 article for *Association Management* magazine:

"Again, where was everybody, especially the so-called experts so many of us depend on? How could all of these well-intentioned boards, auditors, dedicated employees, and analysts—and the financial press—miss the signs that big problems were in this offending company's future?

The financial ripple goes well beyond lost jobs, decimated pension savings accounts, and evaporated stock portfolios. This series of debacles has had a secondary impact on thousands of investors, many of whom do not even realize that they had holdings in such companies as part of their mutual funds.

While we speculate as to whether the people involved in the day-to-day operations were incredibly stupid or intentionally

---

48 Losey, "Free Enterprise Is Everyone's Responsibility," *Association Management*, October 2002.
49 Ibid.

deceitful, the real question is this: *Why didn't our systems and safeguards protect or, at a minimum, warn the public? Have we reached the point at which only federal regulators can be trusted with this responsibility?*

Of course, legal penalties imposed on corporate officers found guilty of illegal practices are important and should be continued aggressively! However, as we have seen, in many cases, executives are less likely to go to jail, or to stay in jail as long as someone else who steals an old, beat-up Chevy.

We all share some responsibility to protect and reinforce our free-enterprise system. Even modest but visible and symbolic actions can convey that we, as participants in and beneficiaries of the free-enterprise system, do not like what has happened and will not let those responsible off the hook.

For example, is the local chamber of commerce membership department inclined to merely send out the annual dues invoice to a member company proven guilty of fraud? Why not encourage the local or national chamber board to contact the wayward corporation and ask why the company membership should not be suspended or canceled?

What about trade association violators? Will they be handled similarly? Will the complying certified public accountants and attorneys who are as outraged as I am insist their member violators be expelled from their professional organizations and lose their licensure?

At many country clubs, members who do not wear a collared shirt, who play golf too slowly, or who take a big divot without replacing it can be severely reprimanded, regardless of who they are. But what happens when the same executive takes a "divot" out of the confidence in our free-enterprise system? Do we still see him or her on the first tee?

In most police departments, good officers feel honor-bound to report colleagues who violate the code of conduct. Don't we, as the men and women who lead and benefit from our free-enterprise system, have a similar obligation to show our disapproval? Should we not be objecting in any reasonable way we can when we see a company or its officers violating written and unwritten business ethics practices?"

Is It Legal? Is It Ethical?

A common way of defining "ethics" is "rules of behavior based on ideas about what is morally good and bad."[50] The challenge is the people who rationalize their behavior to suit their individual, or group, needs and desires.

Also a challenge is separating what is legal and what is ethical, since merely being legal does not make something necessarily ethical, and sometimes what is considered ethical behavior is not necessarily legal.

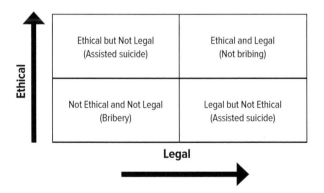

The following shows how alternatives range from what is very illegal and unethical to what is very legal and ethical. But

---

50 "Ethic," http://www.merriam-webster.com/dictionary/ethic.

note, there can also be situations in which something is legal but not ethical or ethical and not legal.

As illustrated above, assisted suicide is considered ethical by some in jurisdictions where it is not legal. In jurisdictions where assisted suicide is legal, others nevertheless consider assisted suicide unethical. Too often the only test used is, "Is it legal?" That may not, in some cases, be a sufficiently high enough standard.

"The responsibility for the front-line defense of our free-enterprise system rests with us as leaders. We must audit and sanction not only our own offending employees but also the rascal executive. The free-enterprise system and our way of life are too important for us to do anything else."[51]

---

51 Losey, "Free Enterprise Is Everyone's Responsibility," *Association Management*, October 2002.

CHAPTER 18

Leadership Made Simple, Not Easy

If I were to list just the titles of the books dedicated to the subject of leadership, I could probably add another one hundred pages to this book.

Yes, leadership is important—critical, in fact. No organization can long exist without good leadership.

Leadership is the capacity to influence others to jointly work toward a specific goal. Key elements are recognizing change and solving problems, which are what we get paid to do. Key skills, abilities, and diversified experience are necessary to:

- Identify and define the problem.
- Generate alternative solutions.
- Evaluate the alternative solutions.
- Determine the "best" solution.
- Take actions to "mitigate" the disadvantages of the best solution.
- Implement the decision.
- Follow up to evaluate the success of the solution.
- Take corrective action, where necessary.

After all, if we never experienced change, we would not need leaders.

Someone once told me that there are only two types of people who like "change": One is a baby with a wet diaper, and the other is a cashier working at a cash register.

However, change always happens, sometimes at different frequencies and impact. The desired result is making things happen to address the changes—in the right way. Major contributors to doing the right things are the leader's initiative, creativity, interpersonal skills, and values.

Consistent with attempting to keep this simple, the execution of good leadership can be greatly enhanced with what I call "The Five I's."

Intelligence

Already referenced, intelligence is the ability to acquire and apply knowledge and skills. We are born with most of our capacity and potential for performance in this area. An appropriate education adds to intelligence. The result is thinking and solving problems with what you know.

Initiative

Initiative is simply doing something without being told to do so. In a competitive environment, high-performing leaders are always trying to anticipate what will be required next versus awaiting instruction.

Innovation

In addition to taking the initiative when others may not, the capacity to offer completely new ideas and better solutions that meet changing requirements is a skill that is very important in a leader. Of course, intelligence and experience will contribute greatly to this skill. However, being innovative requires more than those attributes. It requires a discipline to be not only curious but also willing to challenge and create through dedicated effort.

Integrity

Being honest and having strong moral principles are not automatic. In difficult situations, a reputation for honesty and fair dealings can provide protection when almost everything else fails. Good leaders make their position clear, even if it is contrary to the consensus of others. In addition, they tell the story the same way every time; otherwise, they risk trying to remember what they told someone previously and where. This is easily accomplished if the leader always tells the truth. In the long term, this straightforward, non-contrived behavior will contribute greatly to the credibility critical in any leadership capacity.

All of these characteristics, when combined with sufficient effort, can create a great leader. However, absent effort, mediocrity is a result. I have never seen a successful leader who did not apply significant effort.

In addition to effort, there is perseverance. Sometimes this occurs when a superior ignores, or worse—rejects, a leader's repeated attempts to influence or advance a proposal. As emphasized earlier, high-potential leaders who are knocked down will not stay down. They return time and time again to advance what they believe is a good suggestion. Are they at risk? No, not if they have the skill to continue sincerely and skillfully advancing their recommendation.

Interpersonal

Potential leaders can possess almost all of the "I's," but if they lack the interpersonal skills to lead and work effectively with others, they probably will not be successful leaders, or at least not as good as if they did have this capability.

Lacking interpersonal skills does not necessarily mean they will fail. It is important to recognize that such people may be best placed in a role that allows them to be individual contributors, with their singular opportunity for contribution, even if it means working essentially alone.

CHAPTER 19

Self-Development

Self-development is self-defining. You develop yourself. The most important factor about self-development is to start now. Good leaders do not wait for some possible future company training program that may or may not meet their self-development needs.

Too many people are initially overjoyed to have gained employment, only to "wake up" seven years later thinking, "If I had known I was going to be in this job so long, I would have started to get serious about my career sooner."

In other cases, even high-potential individuals may contribute meaningfully to their organization's tactical and strategic planning; however, at the same time they may postpone or ignore their own personal career planning.

Career development planning contributes to:
- Improved levels of performance in a current job.
- Promotion.
- Becoming a candidate for recruitment by another organization.
- Increased job satisfaction.
- Achieving self-actualization.

- Essential elements of self-planning are to:
- Stay professionally current.
- Assume organizational change.
- Determine your aspirations.
- Ensure your employer knows your aspirations.
- Plan your finances so that you build your own "golden parachute."

New employers appear; current ones grow, adjust as required, sometimes fail or merge, get sold, or acquire new organizations. Very few individuals are lucky enough to be employed by an organization that is successful for their entire working career. Even if that is the case, that organization will have changed dramatically.

The individual must change also or be left behind, missing new opportunities within the organization and elsewhere. Even worse, there is the risk of being terminated if it comes to who stays and who leaves.

No reasonable person would avoid an employer-sponsored development program that would, in some way, contribute to keeping the person current, and even better, expand his or her capabilities. More important than selecting from an employer's menu of developmental opportunities is giving serious thought to your needs and to training opportunities you should independently seek, depending on your situation.

This is very much like investing in yourself. Successful people do it all the time. Not every day, of course, but regularly, possibly a couple of times a year. This is when they take time out to examine, for instance, their personal financial balance sheet and try to plan what needs to change: how to increase assets and decrease liabilities resulting in an increase in net worth.

Achieving a reasonable level of financial independence (sufficient cash and other assets to assist in the event of job loss) will do more to improve an individual's performance than almost anything else. Performance need not be compromised by secondary considerations such as impact on one's job security. This is especially true when dealing with possible difficult ethical situations in a very competitive environment. Lack of personal financial resources may negatively affect the independency of judgment needed when faced with demanding ethical challenges.

Thus, individuals should also consider their personal capabilities balance sheet. What are their "assets," or strengths, and what are their "liabilities," or weaknesses? Maintaining and improving the strengths and decreasing the weaknesses through self-development are the keys.

Any personal analysis should not only include a review of an individual's strengths and weaknesses but also a related plan of self-development. Such self-development must be linked to aspirations. Too often the employee is hesitant to share aspirations and long-term interests. How will self-disclosure of the person's aspirations be received by the boss? Also, frequently the boss is fearful of inquiring about a person's aspirations because of unrealistic expectations the subordinate may develop.

The real challenge is to have both the employer and the employee benefit by having a clear understanding of and appreciation for the employee's aspirations. Customarily, this discussion would be held when the manager reviews the employee's performance against stated objectives. Then also discussed is the subject about the employee's aspirations. If the employee fully understands the requirements of the position he or she seeks, the manager can then initiate a personalized development plan.

Perhaps the biggest advantage to knowing employees' aspirations is that the employer can create an inventory of individuals used in, for instance, succession planning for specific positions.

When I served as vice president of HR for New Holland during the construction of a large manufacturing complex in Brazil, we did not feel that we could fill the general manager's position from our existing management. Therefore, we went to another division within the company, Vickers in this case, and recruited one of its executives for our position.

As soon as we made the announcement of the selection, what would have turned out to be an excellent candidate from our own division shared his disappointment that we had not considered him for the position. He was one of our existing plant managers with great experience and performance.

Why didn't we consider him? We had assumed he would not be interested. It was a major error caused by a failure to "inventory" candidates and their aspirations.

Shortly thereafter, we revised our performance review and management succession program to include a discussion on aspirations. It worked well. So well, in fact, that at the next meeting of the Sperry division HR vice presidents, I shared with the other HR division heads what we had done. Expecting kudos, I instead got a hard slap on the hand. The corporate HR vice president told me that our division could not move ahead unilaterally with this approach.

I was not only disappointed—I was upset. One of my mentors, Harold Dahl, from the Great Neck defense division, pulled me aside and told me I only did one thing wrong. I should have just implemented the change and not worried about sharing a new program with the larger corporation. A rather high price to pay, I thought.

I went back to our division and did not discontinue the program. I just quit talking about it.

Later that year, consistent with the requirement to do so, the president of our division and I went to our Sperry New York headquarters to review with the chairman and other key officers of the corporation our division's succession plan.

I had not told my boss, our division president, about my scolding from the corporate headquarters senior HR VP and his sensitivity to the "aspirations" topic. Nor was the employee aspirations topic on the meeting agenda, and I did not intend to bring it up either. However, my boss, our division president, did. He explained how we were now including discussions about individuals' aspirations and trying to match those aspirations to possible future job assignments.

Then, I held my breath.

The first person to speak was the chairman of the board, Mr. J. Paul Lyet. He said that he thought the "aspiration" added feature was a great idea. He looked to the senior vice president for human resources—the person who had told me not to use this approach—and asked if this was the practice in other divisions. The senior HR VP confirmed it was not being done yet in other divisions, but that he would see that they were aware of how great the program was working at New Holland.

Terminating Your Employment

Again, very few people will get through life working for only one company or organization. Absent death, there are only three ways to terminate employment: The employee quits or retires, or toward the end of the day, the boss comes into the department and while pointing says, "You, you, and you come with me. We are going to a meeting that you will really like. It is called outplacement."

That is absolutely the worst way to be terminated. No notice. Involuntary. The person must scramble to quickly get a new job since the termination was not anticipated, and last week's paycheck is already spent.

When the terminated individual asks, "Why me?," the boss, HR, or the company lawyer refreshes the person's memory about "employment at will."

Yes, employment at will says that as long as a termination does not discriminate in some unlawful way, the employer can terminate whomever it wants, whenever it wants, for any reason. However, employment at will works two ways. An employee can quit at any time, for any reason.

Self-development can and frequently does include deciding when it is time to leave an employer and go elsewhere.

There can be any number of contributors when voluntarily terminating employment is the best option. There may be a need to gain additional experience, which the individual cannot obtain with the present employer. Terms and conditions may have been changed, affecting the employee in some negative way. The employee may have been "passed over" for other opportunities in which the employee had a sincere interest. There may be ethical issues that have become increasingly difficult to accept. Coming to the conclusion the employer has no future or is possibly at risk of failing completely is a big reason to seek alternate employment.

The only time I have recommended that dissatisfied employees not terminate is when they feel they were overdue for promotion or a pay increase. Wait a few months. Management frequently comes to the same conclusion three or four months later.

The best way to get a job is to have a job. It is much more difficult to convince a prospective employer to hire someone who is unemployed. The question is always this: "Why are you unemployed?" Any individual considering transitioning from a current employer to another employer should take some time. This is very important for reasons unrelated to a continuing income stream. Consider the "zero" probability the position the individual is looking for in another company is available, now, when the job search begins. The key is picking the company or organization, not the job, and taking it from there.

The "Sunday Afternoon" Syndrome

When Fridays always seem so distant, and when at about 3 p.m. each Sunday, you experience a pain in the gut thinking about Monday and the job, it is time to consider quitting the job. How do you get that new job?

Start with a career inventory and appraisal.

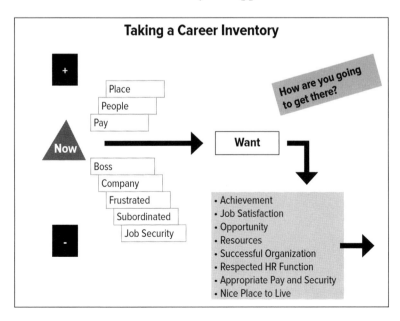

Start with where you are right now. What is your position, and are you comfortable in it? Is your current position a result of a reasonable career progression within your current organization? Identify what you like and dislike about your current job.

I used this approach when I was struggling with the poor results of the Sperry and Burroughs merger to make Unisys. I simply took a piece of paper and sketched out a flowchart as illustrated above.

It was relatively easy to identify what I liked or the pluses of the job. In addition, I enjoyed the community where we lived and did not want to move again after many previous moves. I adored the people I worked with. I respected them and would hate to leave them. My compensation was good; no complaints.

Identifying what I disliked about my current position was not difficult to do, either. I had had four bosses in four years, three with HR experience and one with no HR experience. The new company just did not appear to have the ability to select a senior human resource professional who would satisfy the other top executives and the chairman, Mr. Blumenthal. After the merger, the top HR job always went to a former Burroughs executive. Pre-merger assurances about my future did not materialize. Some of this I brought on myself because of the professional or ethical positions I found it necessary to take.

After twenty-seven years with one employer, it was time to go.

Once the decision was made, the next issue was, what did I want in a job? The number-one desire was a position where I could show what I could do, plus regaining levels of achievement and job satisfaction. I wanted to help advance a successful organization that provided reasonable resources to the profession of HR and respected the HR function. Appropriate compensation and security were secondary. Finally, if I had to relocate, I preferred to live in a metropolitan area with a milder climate and close to water, given my interest in boating.

Once I decided what I wanted in a position, I had to decide: Do I stay, or do I leave?

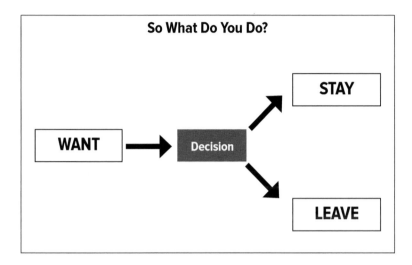

Leaving an employer after many years of service can be tough. The easiest decision is to stay put while taking other actions to minimize the impact of staying. Additionally, I was not so pompous as to believe I did not have development needs. The most important thing, however, was to find a way to test my aspirations against any future opportunities within Unisys. If those actions did not minimize the impact of staying, then I would be forced into seeking another job.

When I was in my thirties and forties, outside headhunters contacted me on numerous occasions. However, especially when I was with New Holland, I loved my job and the people too much to consider any other employer.

Now, four years after the merger of Sperry and Burroughs, the successor company, Unisys, was easy to disrespect and difficult to admire. In addition to what I knew about the Sperry pre-merger hesitation to merge with Burroughs, my own analysis of the situation was that Unisys would continue to experience difficulties. This would make my position even more challenging and, eventually, threaten my job security at a more venerable and disadvantaged age. I had no time to waste. By the fourth anniversary of the Sperry and Burroughs merger, I was 52 years old. It was leave now or increase the difficulty of transitioning to another position later.

The most important thing I did was to start networking outside the company. One disadvantage of working for a very large organization is that too frequently you are networking and exchanging ideas with others in your same organization. Those working in smaller organizations are much more likely to network with professionals from other organizations. Frequently, a more diverse networking involvement yields a better experience.

A good friend of mine, Mike Lotito, noted labor lawyer, asked me to assist him when he was chair of the Society for Human Resource Management (SHRM) labor relations committee. This opportunity led to excellent networking opportunities with the SHRM staff, some board members, and many top-notch professionals.

Now, considering leaving was not so difficult. I listed my strengths and weaknesses, accomplishments, considered what professional contacts I had, and who might be able to help me, or at a minimum, who should know I was ready for a change. I also alerted those whom I hoped to use as future references.

Again, I had a job, and was not immediately at risk, as far as I knew. Therefore, I could take my time, within reason, while being deliberate, looking for my dream job.

What I was not going to do was chase newspaper ads and the Internet postings. I was not going to send out a ton of resumes and then sit by the mailbox to await the rejection letters. I would do a targeted job search of companies I wanted to work for. I asked myself:

- Who did I want to work for?
- Why did I want to work for them?
- Where did I want to work—what part of the country?
- How would I approach the companies I wanted to consider?

Fortunately my networking with SHRM paid off quickly. I was recruited to replace the existing CEO as he prepared to retire. For others, I have frequently recommended the targeted job search approach.

The Targeted Job Search

There is a very big difference between trying to discover "who is hiring" and deciding what organization to work for. Doing a targeted job search is especially effective when the person still has a job but knows it is now time to leave.

Start by creating a list of companies you would consider working for. Then do your research. For instance:

- What was the firm's total revenue?
- Was the firm profitable, and if so, how profitable (return on investment)?
- How many employees does the firm have?
- What is the firm's general reputation in its industry, and among other major employers?
- What is the firm's market share in its industry?
- What is the firm's job security reputation?

- What are the firm's opportunities for continuing education, training, promotion, etc.?

Resumes Are for Rejecting, Not Hiring

In the current business environment, web-based job boards and newspaper ads provide an employer with many more job candidates then it needs or can effectively handle.

Therefore, the HR person or hiring manager usually reviews resumes not to see whom the company can hire, but whom it can reject. HR or the hiring manager wants a pile of a hundred resumes to be reduced to ten or less as soon as possible. All an employer needs is a reasonable number of qualified candidates to make a prompt selection. Thus, the process is frequently more of a rejection process than an employment process, and the "last one standing" (all others rejected) is the one hired.

Untrained hiring managers and HR people can be very arbitrary when going through numerous resumes to fill one job. For instance, I can review almost any resume and reject it—even my own. Examples: Didn't go to the right school, too old (illegal but done every day), too young, too many jobs, not enough jobs, lack of diversified experience, poorly structured resume, not from a similar industry, would have to relocate, worked for a company that has less-than-a-good business reputation, etc.

I would recommend not sending a resume unless you absolutely have to do so. Try to hold your resume until after your first introductory interview. Then you will have established yourself as a person, not just a piece of paper.

In my case, when the SHRM recruiter contacted me about the SHRM CEO position and asked for my resume, I told him I had worked for Sperry, and now Unisys, for 27 years and did not have a resume. I suggested, instead, that he come to the Philadelphia area and we would have lunch.

We had a great lunch with him quizzing me about everything from my education and career to my family and future career interests. He took notes, and later I learned his notes became my resume. I never submitted a resume.

What I did give him was a list of my references. In addition to the names and addresses of my references, I had added what my relationship was with each reference and what that person could speak to in regard to not only my past performance but also my candidacy for the SHRM job.

This I call "leading with your references." No more final line on the resume suggesting, "References available upon request." When I see that on a resume, I say: "OK, give them to me."

Too many hiring managers wait to collect and confirm references until the end of the recruiting process. Why waste time on someone who may not be able to deliver examples of high performance? Why burden company executives with endless interviews with candidates you only think are good candidates? You only have to recommend someone without doing the references first one time, and then have the candidate's references be unsatisfactory, to look really stupid.

For those determined to get a new job, be patient. Again, a key point for job-seeking candidates to remember is the day you approach a company expressing your personal interest in working for it is the day it is not looking for you. The initial chance of approaching an organization that needs someone like you is usually zero. Therefore, be prepared for the initial rejection—you know, the rejection letter that says, "Thank you very much for your interest in XYZ Corporation, but we have no suitable employment opportunities at the present time."

The biggest mistake job seekers make is accepting the rejection and not following up with the preferred employers. I have always advised others in the past to follow up again and again. By doing so, you reinforce your interest in the employer. Find any reason to follow up. For instance, contact a prospective employer about a news article on the company that struck your interest, or remind the employer you still have a job but that your interest in this employer not only still exists but has grown.

The point is that if the chance of an employer needing you is *zero* when you first apply, in thirty days it is no longer zero, and in sixty days the chances are even better. In six months for the reasonably qualified and versatile candidate, the chances of an employment opportunity may be 100 percent.

Remember, when the organization is not recruiting, few hiring managers want to worry about applicants. However, when someone quits, retires, relocates, dies, or is promoted, or business increases and jobs are created, then the hiring manager wants the job filled immediately, if not sooner. And what you want them to do is think of you!

Moreover, remember that employers prefer to offer positions to individuals who have sought them out and have a sincere interest in employment with the firm. They know that such a candidate is much more likely to be more motivated and to accept a position if offered. Employers do not like the candidate who shows more interest in terms and conditions than in the company and the job itself.

I once gave this advice to a young woman who was working at J.P. Stevens, in New York City. She was a college graduate with a degree in textiles, thus the interest in J.P. Stevens. She got a job starting as a receptionist. Unfortunately, after several years, her interest in J.P. Stevens decreased when she was not considered for a more purposeful position in which she could use her special knowledge in textiles. Plus, she lived in New Jersey and had a difficult commute to New York City each day.

She wanted a better opportunity and, if possible, be closer to her home because she and her husband started to plan for children.

I gave her the assignment to search out prospective employers. Johnson & Johnson (J&J) was close to her home in New Jersey and had a wonderful reputation, she suggested. She accepted all of my advice—contacting the company even though no employment opportunities were available at the time, expressing her good-faith interest in J&J, and seeking an initial meeting.

She did get invited to what is considered a courtesy interview: brief but enough time to be seen and make her pitch. She continued to follow up, reminding J&J representatives that she had a job but that since meeting with J&J, she was more interested in employment with the company than ever.

Later, she told me she was reluctant to continue to go back to J&J to reinforce her interest in working for the company. She feared it would offend them. I told her to continue to find reasons to contact them. After all, what could the company do, "not hire you?"

This went on for close to one year, but then, exactly what we wanted to happen did happen. One day, someone got a requisition signed for a new position, or someone retired, quit, or died. The hiring manager's attitude changed from "Don't bother me with job applicants" to "How soon can I interview candidates?

That is exactly what happened to her. A position became available, and the hiring managers quickly rushed to find "that woman who keeps coming back and has a sincere interest in J&J."

She got the job and worked there for more than twenty-five years.

This book is about leadership. Lead yourself!

CHAPTER 20

Michael Revisited

While I was president of SHRM, I was asked to give numerous presentations either at SHRM chapter events or at other professional societies and organizations, corporations, or government agencies. One of my favorite topics was "touching people's lives."

It had been more than forty years since I had seen Michael on the George T. Cantrick Junior High School football field. I had attempted to keep track of him while I also was in school. Then, a few months later, his mother committed suicide. Apparently, when pregnant with Michael, she had been an alcoholic. My mother, who knew her well, suggested that Michael's mother blamed herself for his condition.

Subsequently, Michael's father remarried, this time to a French woman. The new family felt that the best opportunity for Michael was to go to France and live with the new wife's brother who had a farm there. Psychologists had previously suggested Michael should not be placed in a large city environment. Thus, Michael was sent to live in France, also at the time, a country considered more accommodating for people with disabilities.

Michael lived with his stepmother's brother and then spent a period in Belgium. In total, he was out of the U.S. for almost twenty years. So, for many years, I knew Michael was in Europe.

As highlighted earlier, my corporate responsibilities frequently took me to Europe.

One night, while in Brussels, Belgium, three of us from New Holland were in the elevator returning to our rooms. The elevator stopped, and so many people joined us that they pushed us to the back of the elevator.

Then the elevator stopped again, and all of those people got off the elevator but one individual. That individual looked at us and correctly presumed we were from the United States.

He asked us, "Where are you guys from?"

My associate answered, "Pennsylvania."

The gentleman shook his head in acknowledgment but was obviously not from Pennsylvania, and the questions ended.

Then I asked him where he was from.

He answered, "Michigan."

I answered, "Michigan. I am from Michigan."

I asked, "Where in Michigan?"

He answered, "Monroe, Michigan!"

I replied, "I'm from Monroe, Michigan!"

I asked, "What high school did you go to?"

And he answered, "Monroe High School!"

And I said, "I went to Monroe High School!"

I asked, "What is your name?"

He answered, "McIntyre."

I said, "McIntyre . . . I used to go to high school with Charlie McIntyre!"

He responded, "That's my brother! He just got off the elevator!"

At one time, the McIntyres owned Monroe Auto Equipment, the makers of Monroe shock absorbers. They sold the company to Tenneco, but several family members continued with the firm.

The large group had just attended a private dinner related to a European meeting. We all went down to the first floor. The brother and I called Charlie, and he came down to see me.

I was with him long enough to confirm that Michael's father, Mr. Woodward, general counsel of the firm, was also at the meeting. It was too late to call him, and, unfortunately, I had a very early flight the next day, precluding any opportunity to meet with him. I did, however, write a letter to him on the hotel stationery, leaving it at the hotel main desk to be delivered the next morning.

I reflected on the summer I had spent with Michael so many years earlier and how I felt Michael had also touched my life. Mr. Woodward subsequently confirmed that Michael was doing well and how much he and his family appreciated my assistance that summer so many years ago.

Michael Still on My Mind

While I was at SHRM, more than twenty years later, I was also heading up a U.S. Department of Labor special program for people with cognitive disabilities. I frequently advanced the importance of working positively with the disabled. Of course, Michael, my childhood friend, was always on my mind.

On several occasions, at conferences and meetings, I told Michael's story, including seeing him for the last time on the football field and knowing that he not only had been able to stay in school but had played on the football team.

The point was, with a little bit of help and understanding, those with disabilities can accomplish much more than others anticipate.

On occasion, after my presentation, people would ask what happened to Michael. I would have to admit that all I knew was that he had spent many years in Europe, but that I had lost track of him. This bothered me more and more, so I started an effort to find him.

His father had passed away. I knew that Michael had an older brother, Peter, who had long ago left Monroe. Also, with such a common name—Woodward—I had no luck finding the brother. Michael also had a younger sister, but she, too, had left Monroe and married, and I did not know her married name.

I then attempted to contact some of my old friends from Monroe, and they had no information about the family either.

I even contacted someone who had worked for Monroe Auto Equipment for a number of years. He knew the Woodward family and said he thought the only person still in Monroe was Peter Woodward's daughter. However, she too had married, and my contact did not know her name. Still no luck in finding a family member who might know where Michael was.

Fortieth Wedding Anniversary

In 2000, my wife and I were going to return to Monroe, Michigan, our shared hometown, for our fortieth wedding anniversary and to renew our vows. We invited our wedding party and a number of relatives. I called the Monroe Golf and Country Club, where my parents had been longtime members, to inquire if we could host a dinner there.

A very nice woman was helpful, and arrangements were quickly confirmed. Then, for some unknown reason, I offered to the club representative that my father and mother had been longtime members and that I had caddied there for many years as a teenager. After that I added that my father had even been chair of the club's board of directors at one time.

She responded that her grandfather had also previously been chair of the board of directors. I thought I might know him and asked who her grandfather was. She replied, "Mr. William Woodward."

I was stunned.

I immediately asked, "Are you Peter's daughter?" How could it be, I thought simultaneously, that of all the people in Monroe, I found this woman?

I told her I knew Michael and confirmed that Michael was her uncle.

The best news was she knew where Michael was living. She told me that Michael was with a family in Tifton, Georgia. She gave me the phone number.

I could not call.

I was terrified that, after telling the Michael story so many times and feeling so good about how I had helped him, if I called, and he did not recall me or our time together, I would feel terrible.

Finally, I called. Michael was not home. Bobbie Rowan, the homeowner and Michael's administrator, answered. I identified myself and why I was calling. I told them about my search for Michael and how I had obtained their telephone number.

Mr. Rowan and his wife, Thelma, understood immediately, but knew nothing of me. Michael had lived with this wonderful couple since 1980. They made it clear that Michael was considered a member of their family. They encouraged me to call again when Michael was home.

The next day I called again, and this time Michael answered. I identified myself and asked if he remembered me. His response was, "Sure, you went to Cantrick, like me."

We stayed on the phone for a long time bringing each other up to date on what had happened to each of us during those many years apart. Then I made plans to visit him in Tifton. Michael suggested I stop at a certain gas station on the outskirts of Tifton, and he would meet me there and lead me to their home. I had not known that he had made so much progress that he qualified for a Georgia driver's license.

We had a long meeting of reminiscing and catching up on our separate lives. We have met many times since, especially since I relocated to Northern Florida, only a few hours from his home.

A few years ago, I was invited to be a keynote speaker for the SHRM Michigan State Conference in Grand Rapids. Michael had suggested several times that he would like to go back to Michigan and Monroe. He had not been there since his mother died. I asked him to go with me.

His sister, whom by now I had also been in contact with, lived in Atlanta and arranged to get Michael to the airport, and I met up with him there.

We did two major things. One was the speech, and the other was to meet with several people for lunch in Monroe. Invited were close friends from high school, Ron Gruber and Harry Herkimer, who had met Michael when he hung out with our group so many years previously. Michael's brother, Peter, and his daughter, the woman from the country club who unlocked the search for Michael, also attended. Then there was Donna Overmyer, also a Monroe High graduate, and a longtime friend. She brought her husband, Jay.

The coincidences related to finding Michael were not exhausted. I did not know it, but Jay Overmyer was one of Michael's teachers at Cantrick Junior High School. He brought the school's yearbook and shared what he remembered about Michael in the most appropriate way.

The Speech

The speech went well. Once again, my favorite subject was touching people's lives. I closed with Michael's story, but this time, I could tell the whole story and how we had been reunited. I had previously alerted Michael of the subject and the fact I would talk about our longstanding relationship. I asked him if, when I was done, he would like to come to the podium to be recognized. He said he would like to do that.

This time I did not end the Michael story with seeing him from the car, not only still in school, but on the football team.

Michael Woodward returns to Michigan and speaks from the podium.

I shared how I had found him in Tifton, Georgia, and the great reunion we had experienced. Then I announced that he was in the audience and that I wanted to share him with all of them. I called for Michael to come to the podium, and he promptly walked, with vigor, to the stage and podium.

We shook hands and hugged.

He went to the podium and with a loud and confident voice said, "I want to tell you how happy I am to be back in Michigan." There was thundering applause and not a dry eye in the place.

Index

About the Author

Michael R. Losey, SPHR, CAE, is a past president and CEO of the Society for Human Resource Management (SHRM). Before being named to the Society's top position in 1990, Losey previously served 30 years in HR management and executive level positions with two *Fortune* corporations. He has been active in international human resources and is a past president of the North American Human Resource Management Association (NAHRMA) and the World Federation of Personnel Management Associations (WFPMA). He has also served on the board of directors of SHRM, the SHRM Foundation and the Human Resource Certification Institute. Losey has authored more than 60 articles, co-edited *Tomorrow's HR Management* (John Wiley & Sons, 1997) and *The Future of Human Resource Management* (John Wiley & Sons, 2005). He has previously testified in Congress on pending workforce and labor issues.

Additional SHRM-Published Books

View from the Top: Leveraging Human and Organization Capital to Create Value
Richard L. Antoine, Libby Sartain, Dave Ulrich, Patrick M. Wright

California Employment Law: An Employer's Guide, Revised & Updated for 2017
James J. McDonald, Jr.

101 Sample Write-ups for Documenting Employee Performance Problems: A Guide to Progressive Discipline & Termination, Third Edition
Paul Falcone

Developing Business Acumen SHRM Competency Series: Making an Impact in Small Business HR
Jennifer Currence

Applying Critical Evaluation SHRM Competency Series: Making an Impact in Small Business HR
Jennifer Currence

Touching People's Lives: Leaders' Sorrow or Joy
Michael R. Losey

From Hello to Goodbye: Proactive Tips for Maintaining Positive Employee Relations, Second Edition
Christine V. Walters

Defining HR Success: 9 Critical Competencies for HR Professionals
Kari R. Strobel, James N. Kurtessis, Debra J. Cohen, and Alexander Alonso

HR on Purpose: Developing Deliberate People Passion
Steve Browne

A Manager's Guide to Developing Competencies in HR Staff
Phyllis G. Hartman

Tips and Tools for Improving Proficiency in Your Reports
Phyllis G. Hartman

Developing Proficiency in HR: 7 Self-Directed Activities for HR Professionals
Debra J. Cohen

Manager Onboarding: 5 Steps for Setting New Leaders Up for Success
Sharlyn Lauby

Destination Innovation: HR's Role in Charting the Course
Patricia M. Buhler

Got a Solution? HR Approaches to 5 Common and Persistent Business Problems
Dale J. Dwyer & Sheri A. Caldwell

HR's Greatest Challenge: Driving the C-Suite to Improve Employee Engagement and Retention
Richard P. Finnegan

Business-Focused HR: 11 Processes to Drive Results
Shane S. Douthitt & Scott P. Mondore

Proving the Value of HR: How and Why to Measure ROI, Second Edition
Jack J. Phillips & Patricia Pulliam Phillips

SHRMStore Books Approved for Recertification Credit

Aligning HR & Business Strategy/Holbeche, 9780750680172 (2009)

Becoming the Evidence-Based Manager/Latham, 9780891063988 (2009)

Being Global/Cabrera, 9781422183229 (2012)

Best Practices in Succession Planning/Linkage, 9780787985790 (2007)

Calculating Success/Hoffmann, 9781422166390 (2012)

Collaborate/Sanker, 9781118114728 (2012)

Deep Dive/Horwath, 9781929774821 (2009)

Effective HR Management/Lawler, 9780804776875 (2012)

Emotional Intelligence/Bradbury, 9780974320625 (2009)

Employee Engagement/Carbonara, 9780071799508 (2012)

From Hello to Goodbye/Walters, 9781586442064 (2011)

Handbook for Strategic HR/Vogelsang, 9780814432495 (2012)

Hidden Drivers of Success/Schiemann, 9781586443337 (2013)

HR at Your Service/Latham, 9781586442477 (2012)

HR Transformation/Ulrich, 9780071638708 (2009)

Lean HR/Lay, 9781481914208 (2013)

Manager 3.0/Karsh, 9780814432891 (2013)

Managing Employee Turnover/Allen, 9781606493403 (2012)

Managing the Global Workforce/Caliguri, 9781405107327 (2010)

Managing the Mobile Workforce/Clemons, 9780071742207 (2010)

Managing Older Workers/Cappelli, 9781422131657 (2010)

Multipliers/Wiseman, 9780061964398 (2010)

Negotiation at Work/Asherman, 9780814431900 (2012)

Nine Minutes on Monday/Robbins, 9780071801980 (2012)

One Strategy/Sinofsky, 9780470560457 (2009)

People Analytics/Waber, 9780133158311 (2013)

Performance Appraisal Tool Kit/Falcone, 9780814432631 (2013)

Point Counterpoint/Tavis, 9781586442767 (2012)

Practices for Engaging the 21st Century Workforce/Castellano, 9780133086379 (2013)

Proving the Value of HR/Phillips, 9781586442880 (2012)

Reality-Based Leadership/Wakeman, 9780470613504 (2010)

Social Media Strategies/Golden, 9780470633106 (2010)

Talent, Transformations, and Triple Bottom Line/Savitz, 9781118140970 (2013)

The Big Book of HR/Mitchell, 9781601631893 (2012)

The Crowdsourced Performance Review/Mosley, 9780071817981 (2013)

The Definitive Guide to HR Communications/Davis, 9780137061433 (2011)

The e-HR Advantage/Waddill, 9781904838340 (2011)

The Employee Engagement Mindset/Clark, 9780071788298 (2012)

The Global Challenge/Evans, 9780073530376 (2010)

The Global Tango/Trompenaars, 9780071761154 (2010)

The HR Answer Book/Smith, 9780814417171 (2011)

The Manager's Guide to HR/Muller, 9780814433027 (2013)

The Power of Appreciative Inquiry/Whitney, 9781605093284 (2010)

Transformative HR/Boudreau, 9781118036044 (2011)

What If? Short Stories to Spark Diversity Dialogue/Robbins, 9780891062752 (2008)

What Is Global Leadership?/Gundling, 9781904838234 (2011)

Winning the War for Talent/Johnson, 9780730311553 (2011)